Holding on and hanging in

LORNA MILES

ADOPTION
& FOSTERING

Published by
British Association for Adoption & Fostering
(BAAF)
Saffron House
6–10 Kirby Street
London EC1N 8TS
www.baaf.org.uk

Charity registration 275689 (England & Wales)
and SC039337 (Scotland)

© Lorna Miles, 2010

British Library Cataloguing in Publication Data
A catalogue record for this book is available from
the British Library

ISBN 978 1 905664 78 8

Project management by Jo Francis, BAAF
Cover design by Helen Joubert
Designed by Andrew Haig & Associates
Typeset by Fravashi Aga
Printed in Great Britain by T J International
Trade distribution by Turnaround Publisher Services, Unit 3,
Olympia Trading Estate, Coburg Road, London N22 6TZ

BAAF is the leading UK-wide membership organisation for all
those concerned with adoption, fostering and child care issues.

The paper used for the text pages of this book is FSC certified.
FSC (The Forest Stewardship Council) is an international network
to promote responsible management of the world's forests.

Printed on totally chlorine-free paper.

FSC

Mixed Sources
Product group from well-managed
forests and other controlled sources

Cert no. SGS-COC-2482
www.fsc.org
© 1996 Forest Stewardship Council

Contents

Acknowledgements

To Tim, David and Malcolm: I may have written the book but we are a team and we would have achieved nothing if we hadn't done this together. Thank you for all the times you have taken the blame when it wasn't your fault, for the cups of tea and boxes of tissues that appeared just at the right moment, and for being able to maintain a sense of humour even in the darkest times. Humour has been our lifeline.

To all of Wayne's team past and present: I know that you have always done your best. Like us, you have had to work within a system that doesn't always lend itself to meeting the needs of the child – particularly those as traumatised as Wayne. Setting up the therapeutic fostering scheme has been a brave attempt to make a significant difference to some of the most damaged children's lives – thank you for having the courage to give it a go; only time will tell what the outcomes will be.

I am also grateful to BAAF for giving me the chance to write this book, Elaine Dibben for her comments, and to Hedi Argent for her support and for helping me to tell our story in my way.

There are a few "special" friends and family members who have given us huge support in many ways – you will know who you are – thank you.

About the author

Lorna Miles has been married to Tim for 32 years and has two adult adopted sons, David and Malcolm. Lorna and Tim live in a village on the edge of the Cotswolds and have been involved with children in the care system in various ways since 1977 when they became "aunt and uncle" to a young girl in a children's home. Over the years, in addition to fostering at various times, Lorna has worked with children, young people and often their parents or carers in a number of settings, including schools, a youth offenders' institute, community education, a family centre and as a social work assistant.

For Wayne

*You have taught me more than I could ever have hoped
to learn in a lifetime*

The Our Story series

This book is part of BAAF's Our Story series, which explores adoption experiences as told by adoptive parents.

Also available in the series:
- *An Adoption Diary* by Maria James
- *Flying Solo* by Julia Wise
- *In Black and White* by Nathalie Seymour
- *Adoption Undone* by Karen Carr
- *A Family Business* by Robert Marsden
- *Together in Time* by Ruth and Ed Royce
- *Take Two* by Laurel Ashton

The series editor

Hedi Argent is an independent family placement consultant, trainer and freelance writer. She is the author of *Find me a Family* (Souvenir Press, 1984), *Whatever Happened to Adam?* (BAAF, 1998), *Related by Adoption* (BAAF, 2004), *One of the Family* (BAAF, 2005), *Ten Top Tips for Placing Children in Families* (BAAF, 2006), *Josh and Jaz have Three Mums* (BAAF, 2007), *Ten Top Tips for Placing Siblings* (BAAF, 2008), and *Ten Top Tips for Supporting Kinship Placements* (BAAF, 2009). She is the co-author of *Taking Extra Care* (BAAF, 1997, with Ailee Kerrane) and *Dealing with Disruption* (BAAF, 2006, with Jeffrey Coleman), and the editor of *Keeping the Doors Open* (BAAF, 1988), *See You Soon* (BAAF, 1995), *Staying Connected* (BAAF, 2002), and *Models of Adoption Support* (BAAF, 2003). She has also written five illustrated booklets in the children's series published by BAAF: *What Happens in Court?* (2003, with Mary Lane), *What is Contact?* (2004), *What is a Disability?* (2004), *Life Story Work* (2005, with Shaila Shah) and *What is Kinship Care?* (2007).

Foreword

I was delighted, though somewhat apprehensive, when first asked to provide a foreword for this book. Lorna's very personal account of the highs and lows of living every day with Wayne reflects the total commitment needed by carers – and I can't beat that!

The therapeutic fostering scheme was set up with the aim of providing a small group of children and adolescents (just 2.5% of the young people in the care of one local authority) with an effective alternative to residential care. We developed the scheme in response to the needs of a particular child whose foster placement could not be sustained unless the carer could have specialised training and support and was able to give up work outside the home. This had, at the very least, some financial implications but we knew the challenge was greater than just money.

In 2003 a group of care professionals – from social work assistants to senior managers together with psychologists and therapists – met together, to see what could be achieved; our brief was to consider the young person identified but also to build upon the plan for other children presenting with similar needs.

We met many times, consulted with many people and produced seven draft protocols over the next three years – and still we learn and make adjustments! Nevertheless, we have progressed, and have now seen six young people thrive with this style of parenting care. We have also used at least some of the same principles in many more foster placements.

Therapeutic foster care is based on the philosophy that the most positive and enriching environment for most children or adolescents with severe emotional, behavioural and attachment difficulties is within a family home while attending local schools.

One of the strengths of the scheme is undoubtedly that children who would otherwise not experience family life may do so; a further strength is that we are keeping our most vulnerable children within the borough, and this allows access to tried and tested resources and easier communication systems when things "go wrong".

In order to support the scheme, a small but growing number of staff are now trained to work and respond in a therapeutic way – but we have had to learn (often to the cost of carers in particular) that not all professionals can work in this way. In considering the difficulties, I would have to mention the enormous challenge for our local education colleagues, and the fact that the type of education needed for this group of children cannot easily be provided within the state system. I believe that the social work and psychology services, which began planning for the scheme with such enthusiasm, would have done better to include our education service at a much earlier stage: we could then have learned together to avoid expectations of the impossible.

Financially, the scheme has had to take its place amongst other services competing for funds and this will always remain a problem. Any agency embarking on such a project – beware: whatever the bold figures, this is not a "cheap option" compared to residential care. Furthermore, what some regard to be a young person's or carer's right seems to others like a luxury, and this has created real tensions between key players.

The greatest challenge – and one that we had all hugely underestimated – has been the provision of regular and quality respite arrangements. We have advertised, approached independent providers and tried to "home grow" families who can offer this essential ingredient – and so far have failed miserably. This lack of provision has negatively impacted on the progress of the scheme and the wellbeing of all those involved, most specifically on the carers themselves, but also on workers who have often been on the receiving end of impatient colleagues and fraught carers who are tired, frustrated and disappointed that the service has been unable to deliver what they and the young people need.

Finally, do I personally believe we should persevere? Am I convinced we were right to launch the therapeutic fostering scheme? The answer to both questions is "yes". But everyone involved has had to invest many hours and a great deal of emotional energy; each one of us has had to find their own personal support in order to keep going. Perhaps a scheme like this requires a stronger framework than we have yet been able to provide.

The carers have been amazing and I have learned a lot from them, but my greatest admiration is for the young people themselves: youngsters who were so traumatised by early experiences that they had cut off from their emotions. I have watched each one of them bravely learn that some adults can be trusted, and that it is OK to revisit painful memories – with the promise and hope of a better future.

Fostering manager attached to Wayne's local authority therapeutic fostering scheme
September 2009

Introduction

Time

Once upon a time, there was an island where all Feelings and Qualities lived – Happiness, Sadness, Knowledge, and all of the others, including Love.

One day it was announced that the island would sink, so all the Feelings repaired their boats and sailed away. Love was the only one who stayed.

Love wanted to persevere until the last possible moment. When the island was almost covered by water, Love decided to ask for help. Richness was passing by in a grand boat. Love said, 'Richness, can you take me with you?' Richness answered, 'No, I can't. There is a lot of gold and silver in my boat. There is no place here for you.'

Next, Love decided to ask Vanity who was also sailing by in a beautiful vessel. 'Vanity, please help me!' 'I can't help you, Love. You are all wet and might mess up my boat,' Vanity answered.

Sadness was close by, so Love said, 'Sadness, let me go with you, please.' 'Oh…Love,' replied Sadness, 'I am so sad that I need to be by myself.' Happiness passed by Love too, but she was so happy that she did not even hear when Love called to her!

Suddenly, there was a voice: 'Come, Love, I will take you.' It was an elder. Love felt so blessed and overjoyed that he even forgot to ask the elder her name. When they arrived on dry land, the elder went her own way.

Love, realising how much he owed the elder, asked Knowledge, 'Who helped me?' 'It was Time,' Knowledge answered. 'Time?' asked Love, 'but why did Time help me?'

Knowledge smiled and answered, 'Because only Time is capable of understanding how great Love is.'

Source unknown

Sent across cyberspace by a friend who had no idea of the journey our family was embarking on, the above arrived in our email inbox a few days before Wayne's placement started. Its significance for the task that lay ahead didn't escape us, but the inspiration it would provide in the longer term, prompting us to keep going when it seemed that we had taken on an impossible task, was not so instantly apparent.

As parents of adopted twins and as experienced foster carers, my husband Tim and I thought we knew what to expect when Wayne was placed with us under a therapeutic fostering scheme, with a view to remaining with us until he reached independence.

The day-to-day care of children placed under the scheme is based on parenting principles that promote secure attachments and which incorporate an attitude based on playfulness, acceptance, curiosity and empathy (PACE), as described in Dan Hughes' book, *Building the Bonds of Attachment* (2006).

Dan Hughes developed his model for attachment-focused parenting and family therapy over a period of approximately 12 years, working with troubled children and young people who were adopted or fostered. Despite being cared for by "good" parents, in kind and loving homes, these children showed little or no evidence of being able to rely on their caregivers to keep them safe, to help them regulate their emotions or to help them generally understand life and make their way in the world. In fact, the opposite was more often true: these children saw their carers as a source of fear whom they needed to control through manipulation, over-compliance, intimidation or role-reversal in order to keep themselves safe. The caregivers reacted by feeling responsible for the problems the child was experiencing and for not being able to solve them either. They must be failures as parents!

Dan Hughes' method, Dyadic Developmental Psychotherapy, centres around the parent–child relationship and requires ongoing, reciprocal experiences between parent and child. Much has been written on the subject of "attachment" since 1969 when John Bowlby published *Attachment*, the first volume of the *Attachment and Loss* trilogy, but his claim that the key role of the "mother" is to provide her child with a secure base from which to explore is as valid today as it was then, and forms the basis of Dan Hughes' methods. Alongside this, he uses what he terms as the three qualities of inter-subjectivity: attunement – matching the child's state; attending – experiencing the same event as the child but with a different perspective; and working towards understanding the event/behaviour.

On his website, Dan Hughes details the basic principles of his method:

> 1. Eye contact, voice tone, touch (including nurturing -holding), movement and gestures are actively employed to communicate safety, acceptance, curiosity, playfulness and empathy, and never threat or coercion.

2. Opportunities for enjoyment and laughter, play and fun, are provided unconditionally throughout every day with the child.

3. Decisions are made for the purpose of providing success, not failure.

4. Successes become the basis for the development of age-appropriate skills.

5. The child's symptoms or problems are accepted and contained. The child is shown how these simply reflect his/her history. They are often associated with shame, which must be reduced by the adult's response to the behaviour.

6. The child's resistance to parenting and treatment interventions is responded to with acceptance, curiosity, and empathy.

7. Skills are developed in a patient manner, accepting and celebrating "baby-steps" as well as developmental plateaux.

8. The adult's emotional self-regulation abilities must serve as a model for the child.

9. The child needs to be able to make sense of his/her history and current functioning. The reasons are not excuses, but rather they are realities necessary to understand the developing self and current struggles.

10. The adults must constantly strive to have empathy for the child and never forget that, given his/her history, s/he is doing the best s/he can.

11. The child's avoidance and controlling behaviours are survival skills developed under conditions of overwhelming trauma. They will decrease as a sense of safety increases, and while they may need to be addressed, this is not done with anger, withdrawal of love, or shame.

(Taken from www.danielhughes.org/, with kind permission from Dan Hughes)

We had received training from the clinical psychologist, Jane, who would be supporting us in Dan Hughes' methods. She is attached to the local specialist psychological support service for children in care and adopted children, and had trained with Dan Hughes in the USA. She would be a pivotal member of the team supporting Wayne's placement with us. Together with her colleague, Anne, a therapist with the same organisation, she would offer regular consultations to discuss difficulties as they arose and suggest strategies for managing Wayne's behaviour.

Jane had also played an important role in assessing our suitability to foster Wayne using these methods. She explored our own attachment histories in detail – if we didn't feel safe in any given situation, how could we help Wayne to feel safe? If Wayne's anger made us react with anger, how could we help him to regulate his? We had to be able to respond to Wayne's needs appropriately, even at the most critical times. This assessment process sometimes felt very intrusive but we understood the importance of making sure that this was a successful placement for us all; a placement breakdown would be upsetting for us but disastrous for Wayne.

Wayne was aged nine when he was referred to the scheme, the main aims of which were:

1. To provide family-based care for children with severe emotional, behavioural and attachment difficulties, who have experienced neglect and abuse and a number of placement moves.

2. To keep children in their own community, enabling them to maintain positive links with: their family of origin and past foster or respite carers; established educational placements; professionals involved with the child, such as social workers, psychologists, therapists, advocates, paediatricians and other medical specialists.

3. To promote children's relationships with foster carers as the key agents of emotional and behavioural change by providing them with the opportunity to develop potentially secure attachments, to one or two adults.

Anyone meeting Wayne for the first time would have found him a lively, engaging lad, keen to know everything about the world around him. He was tall and slim for his age, with the most beautiful smile you have ever seen. His ability to communicate with adults for a short period of time in a mature and confident way allowed him to hide his difficulties from all except those who knew him well. The truth was that Wayne had suffered severe neglect and had witnessed domestic violence and drug misuse. He had a poor attachment pattern, his educational experience had been negative, and at the time of placement he was being taught in the school corridor by two teaching assistants. He had experienced many moves in foster care since being separated from his parents and siblings. His current placement was at breaking point, and until he was identified as suitable for placement under this scheme, a residential setting had appeared to be the only available option.

Most of the good feelings, including love, had left Wayne's "island" long ago, leaving him angry, fearful and with an overwhelming need to be in control, making it impossible for him to establish a positive, reciprocal relationship. He relished power struggles, thrived on causing emotional or, sometimes, physical pain to others, had a limited ability to control and regulate his emotions, and couldn't ask for help. He had such a negative self-image that he even avoided being praised or recognised as worthwhile, believing that he didn't deserve fun, laughter and "good times". Much of his life was spent completely enveloped in shame. He never "switched off", believing that continuous vigilance (hyper-vigilance) was the only way to survive. Wayne certainly fitted the profile of the type of child the scheme had been designed for.

We realised that taking on a child with Wayne's level of difficulties and caring for him until he reached independence was a huge undertaking, but our twins, David and Malcolm, who were young adults but still living at home, fully supported what we were doing. We had planned to return to fostering after a break to support the boys through their "exam years", and when we heard about the therapeutic fostering scheme we knew that this was the challenge we had been looking for. The fact that the scheme offered children who would otherwise be in a residential setting the chance of a positive family life and hope of living independently in the future really appealed to us; if we could only make a difference to one child, it would be worth it.

Regular respite and annual leave, when we could take a holiday without Wayne, had been agreed as an integral part of the scheme, not only for us to recharge our batteries but to re-group as a family unit. We knew that healing Wayne's trauma would not be a "quick fix" and would take a lot of dedication, hard work and some sacrifices, but we felt that we had a good professional network to support us:

Meg – Wayne's social worker attached to the Children in Care team; later replaced by Joan.

Pam – our supervising social worker attached to the Family Placement team; later replaced by Rose.

Elizabeth – manager of the Family Placement team.

Linda – manager of the Children in Care team.

Jane – clinical psychologist, attached to the psychological support service for children in care and adopted children.

Anne – therapist, attached to the psychological support service for children in care and adopted children.

We were under no illusion that helping Wayne to recover the good feelings that he may have never had, or long ago forgotten, and forming an attachment to us as his "family" would be a slow and painful process, but as we awaited his arrival we felt excited, confident and well prepared.

What follows is a glimpse of the reality of parenting a child in this way, and the emotional cost of putting theory into practice.

1

The journey begins

'...and if you hate me, why don't you just tell me...'

Following a series of introductions, including some overnight stays, it was agreed that Wayne would move to us at the beginning of the school Easter holidays, 2005. This would give him a couple of weeks to settle in before the start of the new school term when he would be taking his place in the specialist behavioural unit of a primary school about eight miles away. We would have loved Wayne to attend the village primary school as David and Malcolm had done, but when I approached the school, the Head seemed reluctant to take him on. She claimed that his year group was full and that we would have to apply to the local education authority for permission, but we suspected that, in a high-achieving school where behavioural difficulties like Wayne's were unheard of, she didn't want him spoiling the school's image. We were also concerned that word of Wayne's behaviour could spread quickly amongst the local parents and he would become ostracised. In the end, it seemed better to keep school and social life apart if Wayne were to have a chance of making friends in the neighbourhood.

Because Wayne had experienced a number of changes of placement and because the plan was that he would remain with us until he reached independence, it was important that we conveyed a message of permanence to him. One way we thought we could do this was to let him play a part in decorating his bedroom so that it felt special to him. We also hoped that giving him some control over his new environment might reduce his anxieties.

We had two bedrooms that were unoccupied, one next to Malcolm's room and one next to ours, and we gave a great deal of thought as to which one should become Wayne's. The rooms were of a similar size but the one next to Malcolm's was directly over the front door and by the stairs. We were concerned that when Wayne was in bed he would become alarmed by hearing the front door opening and footsteps on the stairs, so we chose the room next to ours. This would also enable us to keep an ear open for any night-time difficulties Wayne might experience. It was a decision which we later realised held mixed blessings.

Wayne loved nature and he finally settled on an "under the sea" theme for decorating his room. During his introductory visits to us he helped to paint the walls light blue and to put up a frieze depicting tropical fish and underwater scenes all around the room. He chose a darker blue carpet with a velvety feel and dark blue curtains. We built a unit at the bottom of the bed to accommodate a tank for cold water fish; it had a light in the lid of the tank, which could act as a night light and also enable him to watch the fish if he woke up during the night. After much searching we managed to find a quilt cover and pillowcases with dolphins, and stickers of dolphins that glowed in the dark were used to decorate the ceiling. Wayne loved the finished room and couldn't wait to move in.

He had no concept of time and so the planned two

months of introductions seemed painfully long to him. There were times when we felt he doubted that he was ever coming to live with us and we could understand his point. We thought we were fully prepared for his arrival and just wanted to get on with it. Eventually the long-awaited day arrived and we went to collect Wayne from his previous foster carers with whom he had lived for two years. His cases were packed, ready and waiting in the hallway and Wayne leapt into the car almost as soon as we pulled up. There was no hint of sadness on his part as he eagerly enquired if we were taking his belongings to our house first or stopping to buy the promised goldfish for the tank in his room. His previous carers were in tears, offering hugs, kisses and emotional goodbyes, but Wayne only showed irritation at these delays to his departure.

We stopped off at a garden centre to buy a fish but somehow, we ended up with two, who were to be known as Dic and Dom. To this day we are not quite sure how that happened but it should have been an early warning to us that perhaps life with Wayne wouldn't be as predictable as we believed it would be. However, it was several weeks later when we had to admit that we were not as prepared for Wayne's arrival as we thought!

Trying to recreate the "infant–mother dance", which forms the basis for helping the child to develop healthy attachment patterns, is no mean feat when the child is nine years old and resisting intensely. One of the things that had attracted and interested us in working in this way was Dan Hughes' assurance that carers: '...should not be expected to change basic family routines and interactions to match some child rearing "cookbook".' Well, either he needs to re-write that bit of his book or we hadn't quite "got it", because our well-ordered family life was transformed until we were living in chaos!

Every aspect of our day-to-day life was affected; both going out of the house and staying in was fraught with potential conflict and often aggression on Wayne's part. He challenged everything we did. He didn't want to get up in the morning, claiming that it was really the weekend and we were getting him up to be nasty, or that all the clocks in the house were wrong and it was still the middle of the night. Bedtime was as bad – why were we sending him to bed when it was still light? Or again, all the clocks were wrong. He saw no reason to wash, clean his teeth or, horror of horrors, have a shower, because he 'did that last week'. Everything we gave him to eat was 'disgusting', even if it was something he had previously asked for. He was so anxious that one of us might eat his food if he left the table to go to the toilet that he would often wet himself where he sat, or try to take his plate with him.

Wayne's verbal skills were at a level much below his age; however, he compensated for it with his extensive vocabulary of sexist, sexualised or racist comments, which he was more than happy to share with the rest of the world whenever we went out.

Wayne found it difficult to sleep; when he did "drop off" he had nightmares about his past. For Wayne, we were part of the story, and throughout his nightmares he spoke to us as if we were there with him. We spent many nights hiding from the police, trying to break into boarded up houses or cowering in the corner of the bed as incidents of past domestic violence invaded his mind. It was not only heart-wrenching to watch but also exhausting.

We knew before he arrived that Wayne was "wetting" day and night as well as soiling on occasion, but nothing had prepared us for the volume of urine he seemed to produce at night! If he had a settled night the bed would resemble a swimming pool in the morning, with barely an inch of dry bedding to be found. If he had a difficult night, and we were up comforting him, we would change the sheets before trying to settle him down to sleep again. On a really bad night we could change the bed twice and still have more wet sheets in the morning. Added to this laundry list was his normal day-to-day clothing – more wet or soiled items, and if he had been outside to play, several extra changes of clothes, as puddles and mud were just there to be rolled in. The washing machine was on the verge of a breakdown and the rest of us had nothing clean to wear!

Wayne talked incessantly, repeating himself over and over again. What he was saying often made no sense or was totally out of context from what was going on around him. He would often shout at the TV, and if he couldn't understand what we were saying to him he would just argue that we were wrong. The need for Wayne to keep repeating himself became wearing and was one of the traps which could lure you into his world with ease. The usual responses and acknowledgements to his chat seemed to go unnoticed and it was like living with a stuck record or, in the 21st century, should I say MP3? You reached a point where you just wanted to yell, 'Will you please SHUT UP!', which could then easily be turned, by Wayne, into a full-scale argument.

Wayne also thought that every conversation was about him, and would not believe otherwise. One evening he was upstairs, supposedly asleep, when suddenly he stormed out on to the landing throwing anything within reach and hurling a string of foul abuse, ending with, '…and if you hate me, why don't you just tell me, I'll pack my bags and go…' We were dumbfounded; we had all been quietly sitting in the lounge discussing a problem David had with his boss. We jumped up and went to see what the problem was. By now Wayne was battling to get out of the fortunately locked front door, a bulging pillow case in his hand, which I recognised as one that had gone missing a few weeks previously. Wayne was beside himself now, trying to climb out of one of the small opening windows in the lounge. We felt useless: we had no idea what was wrong or how we could help. David and Malcolm retreated to their rooms leaving Tim and me to wonder aloud what on earth could be troubling him.

Eventually Wayne turned towards us, shouting that we should have just told him if we wanted him to go and not called him grumpy and miserable behind his back. The penny dropped: due to his hyper-vigilance he had been listening in to our conversation from his bedroom, convinced that we were talking about him, not David's boss. Trying to persuade him otherwise would have been impossible, so we acknowledged how sad it was that he had thought we were talking about him, confirmed that we wanted him to stay with us, and suggested that if he insisted on leaving, perhaps it would be better to wait until the morning when it was light. Wayne went back to bed, with the pillow case, which contained an odd assortment of survival rations he had secreted away over the preceding weeks, in case we 'threw him out', by his side.

We were well aware of how much easier it is for the carers to slip into the child's world of chaos than to help the child to feel comfortable in a place that is calmer and more ordered, but just how subtly and quickly this had happened to us was unbelievable. One by one we all fell into the trap and Dan Hughes' warning echoed in my brain: '...Remember that if you become more like your child, you both lose, if your child becomes more like you, you both win...' We had to do something, and fast!

We sent out an SOS to our fostering service. Our supporting social worker, Pam, was very sweet; she had just joined the team and was clearly very maternal and supportive, but she didn't quite understand the level of Wayne's difficulties or the way in which we were working. She had a stock answer to every question: 'Give him a little cuddle and tell him you love him.' That would have been great if we had wanted an earful of abuse or a bruised eye, but as a solution to any of our problems it was useless. In response to our questions about the bedwetting, she told us that 'lots of little boys wet the bed' and not to worry about it. We were well aware that a nine-year-old wetting the bed wasn't uncommon; it was the extent of the problem that was cause for concern.

Our sessions with Jane, the psychologist, were not yet underway and so we took matters into our own hands. I contacted the organisation ERIC – Education and Resources for Improving Childhood Continence – which sent us some information leaflets and also provided telephone advice on the wetting and soiling difficulties; even if their suggestions didn't work, at least we had something concrete to try and didn't feel quite so helpless.

A late night, whispered family meeting also took place. We all agreed that we had to work as a team if we were going to survive and humour needed to be the key. We developed a strategy of making loud slurping noises to warn each other if anyone was being sucked into Wayne's world, which thrived on anger. This also had the advantage of not alerting Wayne, who just thought we were all mad!

It wasn't long before we were able to put our new strategy into practice. We were all in the car on a dreadful wet day, precariously making our way along the motorway, when we were overtaken by a police car with sirens blaring and lights flashing. Wayne immediately started to ask each of us in turn if we had seen it. We all said that we had but Wayne went on and on: 'Did you see the police car, it had its lights on and the siren was going...did you see the police car...?' A few miles later, our patience was wearing thin; there is a limit to the number of ways in which you can say 'Yes, I did'. We were slurping loudly at each other, but Tim was struggling to see the road ahead and was at snapping point. Suddenly inspiration struck: I turned to David and said with a gleam in my eye, 'Did you see the police car...?' Thankfully he grasped what I was doing and after saying 'Yes' turned to Malcolm and asked, 'Did you see the police car…?' Round and round we went until after a few minutes Wayne yelled, 'Will you shut up, you are saying the same thing over and over again, you are getting on my nerves!' We all smiled and nodded; you could see the slow realisation on Wayne's face.

As well as the importance of humour, we quickly realised that the ability to act spontaneously in response to any situation was vital. Like smiling sweetly at the staring throng as you struggle to get the child on to a bus whilst he is kicking, screaming and shouting, 'Get your hands off me, you're not my mum'. Or ignoring the obvious irritation of the "City Suits" as you give a running commentary on every mechanical creak and groan when you take the child on their first trip on the London underground. Who knows, others in your carriage may be comforted by your reassurance that although people do blow these trains up, and yes, you would get crushed if the roof of the tunnel came crashing down, it is not going to happen today!

Most people would probably give you a knowing smile if this type of interaction were going on with a toddler, but when the child is a tall nine-year-old, they will take a totally different attitude, particularly when the child's side of the conversation is littered with expletives of a four-letter kind!

As someone who would have previously thrown away a winning raffle ticket rather than face the embarrassment of walking up in front of a crowd to collect the prize, being out and about with Wayne and dealing with the attention his behaviour attracted was a steep learning curve for me. Any vanity I had about how I was perceived by others had to be thrown aside. I will never forget the expression on the faces of my open-mouthed neighbours as I jumped on to Wayne's small BMX bike and went hurtling past them in hot pursuit as he fled from the house, convinced that a minor misdemeanour would result in physical punishment. Wayne glanced over his shoulder, stopped dead in his tracks and hissed, 'Get off the bike!'

'I can't, you can run so fast I can't keep up.'

'Get off the f***ing bike, you are making me embarrassed…you look stupid.'

'You need to stop running then.'

'What, so you can thrash me?'

'We don't thrash children in our house…You stop running and come home, then I will get off the bike.'

'Well, get off the f***ing bike and I will.'

I had stopped him from running. But Wayne was trying to take control again by making me get off the bike when he said, and I wasn't sure what he would do then. I needed to maintain my position. 'OK, you lead the way and I will follow on the bike; once you are safely in the house I will get off the bike.' Wayne turned and ran home as fast as he could.

We quickly realised that it was no good trying to unpick Wayne's behaviour with him when he was too aroused to engage meaningfully in a conversation: it was far better to wait until things had calmed down and then revisit the incident and try to make some kind of sense of it with him.

The mental effort required to work in this way and keep one step ahead was enormous, and in a very short space of time it became apparent that, far from us taking Wayne on a journey to heal the wounds of his early life experiences, we were on a journey too. A journey that was taking us right out of our comfort zone would test us to the limits and force us to discover capabilities we didn't know we had.

2

Trauma

'Today I *know* you are taking me to the supermarket, we are going shopping and then we will go home again.'

We had only driven about two miles from home when suddenly Wayne, who was sitting next to me in the front of the car, leapt over the back of the seat and was cowering on the floor. Fortunately we were only yards away from a lay-by and I was able to pull over.

Wayne peeped nervously at me through his fingers as I leaned over the seat and noticed that he looked scared.

'You're mad at me.'

'You think I'm mad at you – wow, I wonder why that is?'

'Yeah, your face...you were OK then your face went like it was mad.'

I was frantically racking my brain...the radio had been on, I was enjoying the song being played, what had I done? What had made him think I was mad at him? Think! Think! Then I remembered that just as we were negotiating a roundabout I had realised that I had forgotten to take the meat for tea out of the freezer to defrost.

So this was why Dan Hughes places so much importance on inter-subjectivity. As far as I was concerned, I was happy, relaxed and looking forward to enjoying the latest children's film with Wayne at our local cinema. Wayne obviously had picked up on non-verbal cues I wasn't even aware of.

'Was it as we were going round the roundabout?'

'Yeah.'

'I wasn't mad at you; I was cross with myself for forgetting to take the meat for tea out of the freezer.'

'Yeah, well, it's not my fault; I don't know why you got mad at me.'

'It sounds like other people have blamed you for things that weren't your fault.'

'No, no one's done that, why are you saying that? You're saying about when you hit me 'cause my sister climbed up and broke that thing with the sweets in when you were down the pub. That wasn't my fault and you blamed me then and now you are saying it's my fault again.'

This wasn't the first time an innocent comment or action on our part had triggered Wayne into reliving a past trauma. An instant reaction would have been to argue with him that we had never hit him, didn't know about the "sweet" incident or whatever memory had been brought to the surface, but I knew that arguing with him would undermine his confidence about sharing the experience and could create a distance between us. The best way forward was to be curious about the situation and reconstruct Wayne's account of events into what I thought he was telling me. I knew he would soon correct me if I was wrong!

'I wonder if your mum was at the pub and you were looking after your sister and brothers and your sister climbed up to get some sweets and broke something. When your mum got home you got the blame?'

'Yeah, they said it was my fault.'

'You must have been a very little boy then, I guess you were about four or five. Looking after your younger sister and brothers when you are that age is a very big job, I am not surprised something got broken, but it wasn't your fault.'

Delving further into this incident and risking Wayne's behaviour escalating when we were sitting at the side of a busy road clearly was not a good idea. 'Would you like to sit in the front of the car now or are you going to stay in the back?...The front, OK, I will come round and help you.'

One of the key principles of Dan Hughes' methods is to use what he calls "time–in", bringing the child into close physical proximity in order to create a feeling of safety rather than sending the child into isolation. If Wayne had remained in the back of the car, he might have felt that I had withdrawn from him psychologically as well as physically even though the choice had been his. The principle may seem straightforward but when the child's core belief is that they are bad, persuading them that they are still loveable and that you want to be near them can be a challenge.

Incidents such as these were some of the most difficult to make sense of and deal with; often we didn't have a clue why Wayne was acting or reacting in a certain way. If his behaviour was bizarre, we just had to accept that it was part of a bigger picture, a response to a trauma that had become distorted as time had passed. Kate Cairns gives a good account of this in her book *Attachment, Trauma and Resilience: Therapeutic caring for children* (2002):

> ...the intrusive re-experiencing of trauma may be triggered by events far removed from the original traumatic experience. An abused child may register the sound of a creaking stair as associated with the onset of abuse; later they may have no recall of the

abuse itself, but may be triggered to a traumatic stress response by sounds reminiscent of a creaking stair...A child hears a trigger sound whilst painting ...later the same experience of panic may be triggered by the smell of paint, or the prospect of an art lesson, or seeing the art teacher in the street...

It was always preferable to have Wayne in the front of the car; it was his firm belief that as a female driver it was impossible for me to get us from A to B without his intervention. 'We are turning here, you need to put your indicator on...really you should have changed gear but it will be OK if you do it now...did you miss the turning?' If Wayne was seated behind me, each instruction or observation was accompanied by a tap or prod to make sure I was paying attention!

Wayne's unpredictable behaviour in the car could have led me to abandon making car journeys on my own with him, but as we lived in a rural area bereft of public transport, this would have had a huge impact on our day-to-day living. When Tim was at the wheel, Wayne was so different that I also wondered if, aside from his opinion of "women drivers", there was some other anxiety attached to me driving. The trips continued, but Wayne understood that if he poked me or touched anything on the dashboard, I would pull over and delay our journey. Surprisingly this worked. I say surprisingly, because months later when we were heading off to the supermarket, Wayne revealed what some of his anxiety in the car had been about.

'Today I *know* you are taking me to the supermarket, we are going shopping and then we will go home again.'

'That's right, what do you mean... today I *know*?'

'Because now I trust where we're going, I used to think you were saying we were going shopping but really you were taking me back because you didn't want me any more.'

How do you respond to that? Can you imagine that level of fear every time your carer takes you out in the car? Yet if you think about it, you can see how it would make perfect sense to someone with Wayne's history. Here I am, a middle-aged woman, who would fit the profile for the majority of his social workers, taking him off in the car during the working week. Who knows what he was told or understood as he was first removed from his parents, then separated from his siblings as one by one they were chosen for adoption and, in addition, moving from foster home to foster home? Everything said to him may have been perfectly clear and logical, but what was Wayne's understanding of events? Was it any wonder that each outing in the car with me filled him with terror and drove him to try and take control of the journey?

When we reached the supermarket I didn't immediately get out; I sat in the car with Wayne and cried. I shared my sadness with him about things that had happened in the past that might have led him to believe that I was taking him away. I described what I thought his feelings might have been over the preceding months as we set off on each journey. Wayne remained silent, but I hoped that it would help him to connect with his own inner self.

One advantage of therapeutic fostering is that we are able to adapt our responses to whatever behaviour the child presents – this is not always easy for other professionals who come into contact with children like Wayne.

The telephone rings.

'Mrs Miles, this is Mr Page, Wayne's teacher. Wayne has run out of the Unit and is hiding under a table in the corridor. The Head has tried to get him out but he has just hit and kicked him and won't budge; if he injures the Head, he will have to be given exclusion.'

'He must be frightened – he always goes underneath something or into a place where you can't reach him when he is frightened. Leave him there, get a member of staff to sit near but not so close he will feel threatened. When he feels safe again he will come out. At home we have made him a den with a pop-up tent filled with blankets, cushions and some of his favourite toy cars. If he is frightened or stressed, he goes in there until he is OK.'

'That's all very well at home but he has got to realise that children are not allowed in the corridors during lesson time. If he is not coping in the class then he needs to go to the "Chill Zone" and stay there until he can rejoin us.'

The "Chill Zone" was an area the length of the Unit cordoned off by low screens and filled with cushions, beanbags and the like. There was a CD player with headphones and a range of soothing music, comics, books and a few toys. Children in the Unit were free to move to the area if they felt unable to cope in the class, or the Unit staff would take angry, stressed children there to calm down. For the majority of the children it was fine but it didn't offer Wayne the feeling of being enclosed and "untouchable", which he needed. At this stage he was also unable to make a conscious choice about where to go when "triggered" – he was in "fight or flight" mode.

Even with the provision of the den at home, Wayne would flee to the nearest place of perceived safety and we would then gently coax him into his den. I was worried that if the school staff forced him out from under the table he would take flight or trash the classroom. I started to explain my fears to Mr Page. It quickly became clear that if Wayne had been hiding under a table in the Unit there wouldn't have been a problem, but he had made the mistake of moving out into the corridor, thereby crossing the invisible borderline into mainstream school life where rules had to be obeyed. The Head had instructed Mr Page to ring me in the hope that the threat of his "mother" being contacted would bring Wayne out of hiding. Wayne, of course, wasn't worried.

'So what? What will she do about it anyway?' Wayne's

experience was that mothers take no interest in your life at home, let alone at school.

Thankfully the interlude created by the telephone call gave Wayne the time he needed to come out of hiding and he returned to the Unit after receiving a strong telling-off by the head teacher. Wayne, who was unable to recollect what had triggered the incident in the first instance, seemed confused as to what all the fuss had been about. One can assume that the Head's "dressing down" resembled so many Wayne had received in the past that it had fallen upon deaf ears.

To be fair, anything that happened at school in the confines of the Unit was dealt with swiftly and efficiently. Mr Page was approachable and interested in how we were working with Wayne. He, like myself, was importing publications from the USA on a variety of behaviour management strategies and we regularly swapped books or discussed new ideas. The structure and routine of the Unit suited Wayne and intrusive reminders of trauma from the past seemed to be minimal.

Family life, of course, was less structured; we had basic routines and I am a stickler for meals around the table, but we also enjoyed flexibility and spontaneity, having a laugh, playing a joke and the usual family banter. When Wayne was at home, all of this could trigger flashbacks and unpredictable behaviour. How this contrast between the very predictable routine in school and the less structured routine at home was affecting Wayne wasn't apparent to me until I started to read what I thought was an unrelated book. *Little Angels: Life as a novice monk in Thailand*, by Phra Peter Pannapadipo, tells the real-life stories of twelve novice monks who, like many youths in Thailand, had turned to Buddhism as a last resort to escape horrific childhood traumas. As I read each of the twelve young men's or boy's accounts, I was struck by how the rhythm and routine of monastic life had helped them to focus on the present and had reduced their internal re-living of past events. It all started to make sense to me: Wayne was much calmer at school than at home; most of his trauma had been experienced within a home environment; our home was now the least structured part of his life.

The more I thought about it the clearer it became: we were supposed to be re-parenting Wayne and creating an atmosphere of safety and security but we had overlooked the most important features in an infant's life and one of the key principles of Dan Hughes' method: structure, routine and predictability. Once the connection had been made, it took only a few days to implement a routine so that life ran literally like clockwork. Getting up, going to sleep, mealtimes and everything in between happened according to a strict schedule. The improvement in Wayne's behaviour was amazing but the impact on the rest of the family was also huge! There was no more 'Don't worry if you are going to be ten minutes late, I can delay tea a little', or adjusting the morning bathroom routine to accommodate a change in circumstance; life had to run with military precision or Wayne was back to square one.

Tim, David and Malcolm still had their "outside" life so it was only at weekends that they noticed any significant change, but for me it felt like a bereavement – the loss of my life as I had known it. No clearing away of the breakfast until Wayne left for school; God help me if I needed more than a brief visit to the bathroom at a time when I should have been giving him my full attention. All the preparation for tea had to be done before Wayne got in from school at about 3.45pm. Then he had to become the focus of my attention until Tim got in from work and could either entertain Wayne or get the tea ready. If Wayne went out of the house to play with friends, one of us went with him, so that we could monitor his mood and bring him home again before things went wrong. We had to try and set up every situation to be a success. Those lovely chats, catching up on the day's events over a cup of tea when Tim got in from work, disappeared. Instead I had to write him notes, which sat on the kitchen unit awaiting his return. He replied with convoluted and coded sentences, more notes or a promise to 'talk later'; sadly, 'later' often never came. I felt out of touch with my family and both Tim and I were starting to feel out of touch with our friends. Accepting even those social invitations that included Wayne were more trouble than they were worth in terms of upsetting Wayne's routine and the repercussions that would follow. We either didn't go or went one at a time so that Wayne's routine could remain intact. David and Malcolm were ten months old when they were placed with us for adoption, and we had previously fostered babies, but we had never experienced this level of inflexibility in our day-to-day life. The only thing that kept us going was the huge improvement in Wayne's mental state, which in turn improved our own.

However, there was one aspect of Wayne's trauma that Tim and I still struggled with. This is something Angela Hobday, a consultant clinical psychologist, refers to as "time-holes". In an article published in *Clinical Child Psychology and Psychiatry* in 2001, she states that 'time-holes are distinct from flashbacks as the child in a time-hole may have no conscious memory of it afterwards'. This was certainly true for Wayne: he would go into a re-enactment of a previous experience but have no recollection of it later. The fact that he became unreachable was what made these incidents so scary.

Miraculously, we discovered Claire, who lived locally and who had worked with children with behavioural problems. She felt confident looking after Wayne for short periods and Wayne thought she was great. Tim and I had just finished getting ready for a long-awaited night out with friends. We went into Wayne's bedroom to ask him to get ready for bed before Claire arrived. This was the first time we were leaving Wayne with Claire in the evening, though she had taken him out a few times during the day. I think it may have been the sight of me in my "glad rags" and make-up that triggered Wayne, but really I have no definite answer. As I went into the bedroom he jumped on the bed shouting, 'You don't love me, you hate me...yes you do, you hate me. Fat, that's what I am, fat. I am so fat no one loves me.'

There are many words you could use to describe Wayne, not all of them complimentary, but fat would not be one of them; in fact the opposite is true – he is medically underweight.

'Just look at me, so fat and ugly no one loves me...if I could just get rid of the fat then you might love me.'

Wayne is now standing in his underpants, squeezing the flesh on his thighs between his fingers.

'Fat bastard, fat, fat...if only I could get rid of the fat.'

Tim has joined me in the doorway to Wayne's room but our attempts to communicate with him go unheeded. 'Wayne, it's Lorna and Tim, it's OK, we love you, we are just going out with Ken and Heather for a meal, then we will be home again...it's OK.'

'Fat, fat, if only I could get rid of the fat.' Wayne has now moved towards the radiator in his room. 'Perhaps this will do it...Burn, bastard, burn.' He is pressing his bare flesh against the radiator. 'This won't do – it isn't hot enough.' He fiddles with the controls, trying to make it hotter whilst Tim and I are still frantically trying to communicate with him, but nothing is getting through. We debate whether we should intervene physically and hold him until he calms down but we are worried that he may not realise it is us and it could make him worse.

Suddenly the doorbell rings. We hear Malcolm answer it, Claire comes into the house and Malcolm says we are upstairs. Oblivious to what is happening, Claire calls out, 'Hi-ya, are you OK? Is Wayne getting ready for bed?'

Before either of us can respond, Wayne calls out, 'Hi Claire, I am nearly ready, I've just got to put my pyjamas on then I'll be down. I have chosen a story.'

Tim and I look at each other speechlessly. 'Hold on Wayne, we may not be going out now because you have been really upset and we are not sure that it is fair to leave you with Claire.'

'Upset? I am not upset – I am fine. I've just been getting ready for bed and deciding what story I want.'

'But you got upset about being fat and tried to burn yourself on the radiator.'

Wayne's face was incredulous. 'What are you on about? I've been getting ready for bed; you are not going to spoil it now by staying in. I like Claire and I am looking forward to watching TV with her and then having my story...stop making things up.'

We start to say that we are not making it up but can see that Wayne truly has no recollection of what has just happened. What do we do now? Is it safe to go out? Should we stay in? But that will upset him as he is looking forward to an evening with Claire. There are also only minutes left before Ken and Heather are due to pick us up, so it's a bit late to pull out. We decide to go, having alerted Claire to what has happened, leaving our mobile phones switched on, ready to dash home if required.

We must have been dreadful company that evening as our minds were numbed by what we had just witnessed and, more importantly, by what Wayne must have experienced in order to re-enact that scene. The food was first class but the bitter taste of the evening's events would have soured even the finest cuisine. As soon as the meal was over, we made excuses about Claire having an early start tomorrow, so we mustn't be late, and headed home. We opened the door expecting Wayne to be still up and Claire relieved to see us, but Claire was relaxing in front of the TV and Wayne was tucked up in bed and fast asleep.

Events such as this only ever happened at home, and thankfully not very often, but nevertheless they were scary. Angela Hobday's suggestions for pulling a child out of a time-hole are: 'State clearly who you are, give reassurance that they will recognise as belonging to you and not to a previous situation and explain they are in a time-hole' (2001).

None of this seemed to be very effective with Wayne. So, using the time-hole incident that was diffused by Claire's arrival as a model, we set up an arrangement with some family members, close friends and a couple of our neighbours, that if one of us rang them and asked for sugar, they would come to the house, ring the bell and come in for a cup of tea. Another person entering the scene seemed to jolt Wayne back to the present. The same strategy was also useful if he had flown into a rage and we were struggling to calm him down. On the whole this worked well, without too many questions being asked about why people were required to arrive armed with sugar to take tea with us, but one incident really brought home to me how much we were taking from our friends.

It was a Monday evening and Tim was out at choir practice. It was about 8pm and Wayne was engrossed in a TV programme, so I seized the opportunity to ring Ken and Heather to see when they were available for another night out. Ken answered the phone and as soon as he heard my voice he said 'Don't worry, I'll be there as soon as I can, but it will be a few minutes. I've just come off working nights and have put my pyjamas on as I was going to have an early night.' He promptly hung up before I could say that this was a social and not a distress call; I had to ring back repeatedly before he answered again and I was able to explain. It was great that friends were so willing to respond to our cries for help but it also made me realise that our friendships had become a one-way street. Perhaps inviting some friends round for dinner was the answer. That way we could maintain Wayne's routine and offer hospitality to our friends at the same time.

3

Effects of domestic violence

**'What happened? Didn't you have time to do the
cleaning today? This place is a tip!'**

Ken and Heather, closely followed by Ian and Louise,
arrived at the door bearing gifts: flowers, chocolate and
wine. The evening had been planned with the military
precision that was now becoming second nature. The food
had been prepared ahead and was reheating gently in the
oven or chilling in the fridge. We knew our guests would be
unfazed by any "strange" behaviour on Wayne's part; they
were already used to him and had been asked to arrive
about thirty minutes before his bedtime so that he had
time to get used to them being in the house before he went
to bed. We would then sit down to eat...a perfect evening
lay ahead.

Coats had been hung in the hallway and I ushered
everyone into the lounge where Wayne was watching one of
his favourite Saturday night shows, or so we thought. He
was nowhere to be seen. He must be in the bathroom or his
bedroom...no, he wasn't there, where on earth had he

gone? We called and searched but to no avail, no one had seen him go out of the front door but where else could he be? On the outside I was smiling and making light of the situation, but on the inside I was panic-stricken – how far could he have got in such a short space of time? Thank goodness Ken and Ian were police officers – at least they would be able to get an efficient search started immediately.

Tim came to my side and whispered in my ear, 'Go to the kitchen and look towards the dining room.' I did as I was asked and there, barely visible beneath the drape of our "best" tablecloth, which had been brought out especially for this momentous occasion, were Wayne's slippered feet. Tim discretely alerted everyone and they moved back into the lounge while I went into the dining room and crouched down on all fours by the table.

'Nice tent...didn't you hear us calling you, we didn't know where you had gone, we were worried.' Silence. I joined Wayne under the table, feeling sure that none of the books on fostering had mentioned crawling around on the floor in your best skirt, trying to avoid the dog hairs the vacuum cleaner had missed.

Tim had now joined us; he crouched down and peered under the table, with the tablecloth draped over his head. 'You two look cosy but I don't think there's room for me. Why don't you come out, so we can talk better?'

Wayne's reply was emphatic: 'I am not coming out until the fight is over and I don't think Mum should either or she will get hurt.'

'Fight? There's no fight.'

'No, but there will be when you have drunk all that wine – you and those other men will all have a fight about who is going to have sex with Mum and then she will get hurt...I am staying here and I think Mum should too.'

I was furious with myself – how could I have overlooked the fact that friends to dinner and wine could mean something else to Wayne, and would be a new experience for him in our house. We rarely drink alcohol unless it is a very special occasion or we have guests. I had been so looking forward to this evening, a chance for Tim and me to do something "normal" together with friends; we had lost so much of our previous life since Wayne's arrival and now it looked as if this would be off limits too.

My mind started to run wild. Christmas was months away – but what about our twenty-five-year tradition of inviting friends and neighbours round for drinks and mince pies on Christmas Eve? And then there was the family christening in a few weeks' time; we would have to go because we were godparents. There is bound to be a toast to the baby's health.

I wanted our friends to go home, to shout at Wayne, throw the meal in the bin and just sit and cry.

Five months of frustration and grief for what I had lost or would never have was bubbling up inside me. All of my friends were enjoying a virtually child-free existence now that their offspring had either flown the nest or were practically self-sufficient and were probably at this very moment eating a sumptuous meal in a very nice restaurant with an attentive waiter. I, on the other hand, was sitting under the dining table with a petrified child beside me, a lovingly prepared meal spoiling in the oven and friends abandoned in the lounge. What on earth was I doing?

I signalled to Tim to rejoin the others. Was this it, the moment when I said 'I can't take any more' and we would agree that Wayne had to move on? Tim and I had already been discussing our feelings of isolation and abandonment by the network that was supposed to be supporting us. When we had agreed to become part of the therapeutic fostering scheme, which was very new, we had assumed that the various agencies involved – social services, the psychology service, health and education – would be working with us as a team, sharing a common philosophy, but we were rapidly discovering that each agency had its own agenda and we were caught in the middle of their conflicting ideas on how things should be done. What made it worse was that we felt no one, apart from Jane, believed how bad things were. We got the impression that our supposed support team thought we were exaggerating or making a fuss about nothing. We were confused about who was "in charge" or whose advice we should follow.

We also felt that we were not getting any advice at all on managing some specific areas of Wayne's behaviour. A rigid routine had reduced the invasive thoughts Wayne experienced during the day, but the nightmares and excessive bedwetting were still a problem. He wasn't ever still, couldn't go out of the house without causing mayhem, and if you dropped your guard for a second he would seize the moment to cause chaos. Wayne seemed like "Pandora's box" and the speed at which all the different facets of his difficulties were flying out of the box was unmanageable; if only we could shut the lid and get our breath back!

I was really struggling emotionally with Wayne's attitude towards me. 'Do this, do that, get me a drink' – orders barked as he languished in the reclining chair, feet resting on a footstool. The tone of voice he used had a threatening edge to it and any challenge on my part would result in him telling me in no uncertain terms what I would get if I didn't conform.

Wayne's mother had learning difficulties and suffered from depression. The care of her children had also been adversely affected by her choice of partners, some of whom were drug and/or alcohol dependent. Wayne, and presumably his siblings, had been subjected to extreme physical violence by these men; their mother had been unable to protect them as she too had been a victim of these vicious assaults so it was hardly surprising that any intervention by a male member of my household provoked "macho" mode: fists clenched, Wayne would spar up, trying to start a fight: 'So you think you are a big man, do you...come on then...' Had these words been said to Wayne as he desperately tried to protect his mother?

His mother and the children had lived in a variety of temporary accommodation – in squats and with friends and relatives – in order to escape from these drug and alcohol-fuelled attacks, and there were times when, with huge support from social services, some semblance of normality was maintained, but sadly these interludes were short-lived. We suspected but we didn't know for sure if Wayne had witnessed the alleged attempted strangulation or the alleged rape of his mother by one of her partners. In true PACE style we would show patience, acceptance, curiosity and empathy; we would reflect on how sad it was that Wayne believed this was how women should be spoken to and treated. We continuously reassured him that things were different in our house but detected no change in attitude.

If Wayne and I happened to be in his bedroom when he made one of his demands – 'Open the drawer and get me some socks... not those, stupid, the other ones' – he would create a higher status for himself by standing on top of his cabin bed. Then he would launch himself at me, trying to knock me to the floor, or he would climb from the bed, to the bookcase, to the window ledge and finally onto the chest of drawers, kicking out if I approached him or jumping on top of me if I turned my back.

When arriving home from school, Wayne would often wrinkle his nose with disdain as he surveyed the house.

'What happened, didn't you have time to do the cleaning today? This place is a tip!'

I knew this wasn't true, but it triggered memories from my childhood as my mother would never invite anyone into the house, mistakenly believing other people's homes were far better than ours and that she was in some way inferior. Tim, in contrast, came from a family where the door was always open and friends and neighbours came and went as they pleased, often staying for meals. It took him over 20 years to make me realise that people came to see us, not our home, but Wayne's attitude was making me revert back to familiar habits and I was becoming increasingly anxious about the state of the house every time a routine visit by a social worker was due.

Perhaps Wayne was right? From my position under the table, I could clearly see a layer of thick dust on the rungs of the chairs and an assortment of unidentified objects lurking under the cooker; what on earth would our friends think if this dinner party ever got underway?

I recalled the first time Wayne saw Tim assembling the vacuum cleaner, he got so worked up that we truly thought he would have some kind of fit.

'What the hell do you think you are doing? Put it away, that's woman's work.' He refused to eat anything Tim cooked because it was bound to be disgusting – 'Men don't cook, that's what we've got women for!'; this was despite the fact that everything I cooked was disgusting too.

I had never experienced this kind of attitude or been spoken to in this way before. Even growing up in a very conventional home where my father was the breadwinner and my mother the homemaker, we all showed respect and consideration for each other.

Tim tried to explain that this wasn't acceptable behaviour, that in our house we all spoke "nicely" to each other and shared jobs; that there were no specific men's or women's roles; if it needed doing, we all mucked in and got on with it. But Wayne was having none of it, he declared Tim a "wimp" and warned him of the dire consequences of not 'letting her know who's boss'.

Malcolm and David were struggling with Wayne's attitude too. They found it very hard to tolerate their mother being treated in this way. They were getting upset or angry and couldn't understand why Tim and I were putting up with it. They had obviously heard of domestic violence and, like us, were aware that Wayne had witnessed extreme forms of it, but they couldn't understand why he was behaving like this now, when he had become part of a family that operated in a totally different way. They were also struggling with feelings of guilt. David and Malcolm knew that if they hadn't been removed from their birth family at such a young age, they too might have been forced to live a life like Wayne's. It was clear to us that our sons should have been included in the training prior to Wayne's placement with us, so that they could have a greater understanding of his difficulties, but as they say, 'hindsight is a wonderful thing'.

As a family, we needed time without Wayne to regroup and regain the mental capacity to carry on. But our promised regular respite was nowhere to be seen. We had told Pam, our support worker, that we really needed a break, but she said it was too soon and would give Wayne the wrong message. We said that perhaps if something were booked for the future, so we knew a break was not too far away, it would give us the strength to carry on. We suggested October, another three months away, when we wanted to take David and Malcolm to Paris to celebrate their twenty-first birthday. Again Pam refused: she reasoned that as the planned trip included a visit to Disneyland Paris, it would be seen as rejection by Wayne. We either took him or planned something else; very apprehensively, the trip was booked to include Wayne.

Our main priorities when we brought Wayne into our home had been to maintain an atmosphere of mutual enjoyment and respect, to encourage the pursuit of diverse interests and opportunities and to provide clear, firm expectations of behaviour. Above all, we knew we would have to protect the fabric of our family from the compulsive, oppositional and destructive behaviour Wayne was likely to display. But we were tired, the family atmosphere was becoming strained and our world was becoming smaller and smaller. Hobbies and outside interests were being abandoned and fun was no longer on the agenda. I knew we were all struggling in our different ways. Perhaps I had to be the one with the courage to say that enough was enough...

A small movement beside me brought me back to the present; I glanced at Wayne, who was sitting hugging his knees, a haunted look on his face. He was clearly petrified. I don't know if it was the stark contrast between the deathly white, alabaster-like skin of his face and the vibrant richness of his auburn hair or the baby blue eyes, which looked helplessly at me, but in that moment I saw Wayne at his most vulnerable. A child who was scared witless, a child who, more than any other I had met in my work with children in care, needed me and the love and security I knew our family could give. We had to make this work.

My previous irrational thoughts of the dream life I was missing out on started to take on a more realistic form. Tim and I had never craved the "good life". Except for the occasional special night out, we had always been "home birds"; family had always been the most important thing to us. Both Tim and I had grown up in the village where we now lived and we valued the relative protection the community offered. Many of our family and friends lived in the village too and I knew that it offered the best environment Wayne could hope for to face the traumas of the past and begin to heal. This evening with friends would go ahead, even if it meant Wayne lying upstairs awake until everyone went home. He had to experience the difference in order to start believing that things could be different here. We had to acknowledge, accept and have empathy for his distress and anxiety and then structure the evening to make him feel as safe as we could in a situation that clearly was as unsafe as it could get in his eyes.

'Wayne, I can see how scared and anxious you are. This

is going to be hard, but you have got to trust me. Everything is going to be fine; I promise there won't be a fight. You are going to say goodnight to everyone and go to bed, but we will make sure you are safe. The adults are going to sit down and eat the meal and drink the wine, but nothing bad will happen, and Tim and I will keep popping up to see you to let you know everything is OK. I am not going to ask you if that is alright because I know how difficult it is going to be for you, so I am just telling you what is going to happen. I hope that one day we will be able to have friends round for a meal and drink wine and you won't be worried about what is going to happen, but today I know you are scared and that makes me sad. I am sad because some really bad things must have happened to you in the past to make you this scared, but I promise you will be safe.'

I didn't give Wayne a chance to respond, I just took him by the hand, led him out from under the table and got everyone to say their goodnights. I then took him upstairs and tucked him up in bed. Every ten or fifteen minutes Tim or I would pop upstairs to reassure him that all was well and describe what was happening downstairs. We told him which part of the meal we were eating – 'It's the pudding next' – hoping that this would give him a sense of time and an indication of when the ordeal might be over. We also shared some of Ken's anecdotes about the new police dog he was training, called Max. Max was a German Shepherd. He looked tough and fierce like a good police dog should, but he was a young dog and sometimes he too was scared. He bolted behind Ken's legs every time he was faced with a criminal and much preferred playing, stalking cats or digging holes to being a working dog. It would take time for him to learn to trust Ken to keep him safe. Wayne was amused by these tales and we hoped that he might also be reassured by the similarities between Max and himself.

Despite the interruption of our frequent visits upstairs

and the wobbly start, an enjoyable evening for the adults passed without further incident.

As Tim and I lay in bed that night we couldn't help but wonder if Wayne would lie awake all night waiting for Ken or Ian to return in fighting mood. Had we got it right? Should we have gone ahead or should we have cancelled? We both felt dreadful about what it must have been like for Wayne, lying rigidly in bed waiting for the fight to begin, whilst we were enjoying ourselves. But we did feel that it had been the right decision, and that slowly, step by step, Wayne would start to trust us and know that if we said it would be alright, then it would be. However, two things were very clear to us: firstly, that Wayne's place was with us; and secondly, that we had to insist on getting the support and guidance we needed to make this placement work.

The following day was Sunday so there was lots of time for us to reflect with Wayne on how well the evening had gone: there had been no fights, the house was intact and the only "bad" thing was the pile of dirty crockery stacked above the overflowing dishwasher. Wayne made no comment but the look in his eye was one of suspicion, as if last night had been some kind of trick to lull him into a false sense of security. We were discovering that we would have to go over the same ground with Wayne many times before he could start to believe that the life he had experienced so far was not the norm.

By Monday morning Tim and I had agreed that I would contact Elizabeth, Pam's manager, and tell her how we were feeling about the level of social work support. We had never complained about a "professional" in this way before and my heart was in my mouth as I anxiously dialled the number. But Elizabeth quickly reassured me that I had been right to ring. She was sorry to hear of the difficulties we were experiencing, but she also had news to share with us. Pam had decided that she wasn't suited to life on the Family Placement team and had handed in her notice.

Elizabeth would become our supervising social worker until a replacement could be found; this would also give her a chance to listen to our other concerns about the scheme and try to find some solutions. Tim returned home that evening to find me more positive about our future with Wayne than I had been for weeks.

4

Attachment behaviours

**...the only flesh visible when I looked at Wayne was a
streak across his face where he had spread snot
across it...**

'Are you OK, Mum?' David asked as he peered around the
lounge door. Returning from a night out, he had noticed the
light still on which, given that it was the early hours
of the morning, was surprising. He had expected to find
only a forgotten light burning; instead he saw me in my
pyjamas, legs in the air, hanging upside down from the sofa!

'I am fine,' I said, though I probably didn't sound it as by
now I was beginning to feel a little strange and disorientated.
My neck was bent at an angle making it difficult for me to
talk.

'So what exactly are you doing...?' David tentatively
enquired.

I had realised some time ago that this was a mistake as
I couldn't quite work out how I was going to get up again;
sliding down to the floor had seemed the only option until
David arrived.

'Help me up and then I will tell you.'

A few minutes later, clutching the cup of tea that David had made and with my head slowly clearing, I explained that I had been unable to sleep because I was puzzling over why Wayne had so far spent the majority of the summer holiday doing what I had been doing – hanging upside down from the sofa.

I had anticipated that the school holidays would be difficult and that Wayne would find it hard to adjust to the loss of structure and routine, but I was also hopeful that, with careful planning, it could be a time when we would share activities to help with the attachment process. I had stocked up on art and craft materials, checked that the bikes were in good order and had made a mental list of games and things we could do together. But so far all Wayne had managed to do each day was get showered and dressed after the now familiar moans and groans about wasting water, having had a wash yesterday and his clothes being too small as he tried to pull them on over his wet body, with his towel still hanging on the radiator unused. He would then eat his breakfast at speed before rushing to turn on the TV, and hang upside down from the sofa for the rest of the day. The only things that would entice him away were food and his need for frequent visits to the toilet. I had decided to give it a go myself to see if it would help me to understand why it seemed so important to Wayne, but I was none the wiser. I invited David to give it a try to see if he could gain a better insight, but he decided that the few beers he had drunk earlier and hanging upside down probably were not a good combination. David and I chatted for a while, exploring various ways to try and engage Wayne, but all we came up with was writing out a list of each day's activities so that he would know in advance what the plans for the day were.

As I climbed into bed an hour or so later I felt quite proud of the list I had produced for the following day.

Wayne struggled to read, but with the help of "clip-art" on the computer, I had inserted a picture next to each activity so that he could tell at a glance what we were going to do: get up, have a shower, eat breakfast, walk the dogs, have a drink and a biscuit, paint and so on. Pictures worked well with Wayne. I had previously made a similar chart for his bedtime and morning routines, including the order to put his clothes on, as in the early days he would frequently pull on his pants over his trousers and have a major tantrum when asked to change them round.

By the time Wayne was eating his breakfast the next morning, I was starting to feel quite smug. We were ticking the list off as we went along and so far not one word of complaint. The plan for the day allowed Wayne to watch TV after breakfast to give me time to tidy the kitchen and do a few chores before walking the dogs, and I hummed with quiet satisfaction as I wiped down the kitchen worktops. Suddenly the skies darkened and within minutes rain was pouring down.

'Oh dear, Wayne, we can't take the dogs out in this rain, we will get soaked. Don't worry, we will do the painting first and then take the dogs out.'

'But it says take the dogs out, then I get my drink and biscuit, THEN we do the painting.'

'Yes, I know, but we can't go out in this rain, we will do the painting and hopefully the rain will have stopped by then so we can take the dogs out.'

'But you said we would do what it said on the list...'

'I know I said that, we are doing the things on the list, we are just doing them in a different order because it's raining.'

'But it says...' Wayne was pushing the list in my face and pointing at the symbol for walking the dogs. Clearly this conversation was going nowhere. In my attempt to avoid spending hours trying to get Wayne off the sofa and away from the TV, I had completely overlooked one of the key issues for children with attachment difficulties: their need to be in control of events and objects in their lives.

Like countless other children from similar backgrounds, Wayne's life experience so far had taught him that he was responsible for his own safety; you certainly couldn't rely on adults, and in particular not on parents, to do that for you. Because these children have been unable to rely on their primary carers, they often operate within a framework of rigid thought and repetitive actions; they cannot regulate their feelings and have no "middle ground" between their highs and lows. This was certainly true of Wayne: his temper could go from zero to out of control in seconds with few if any warning signs. It became very wearisome when social workers and therapists asked us to take note of the "signals" when Wayne was about to "blow". There were none. We could be having a lovely time one minute and be on the receiving end of his violent temper the next, without any warning in the middle.

Wayne continuously told us and everyone else he came into contact with what was best for them and exactly what they should do. He enjoyed DIY with Tim but ignored the fact that Tim was a builder and knew what he was doing. If Tim asked for a hammer, for example, Wayne would pass something else and argue that it was far better for the job. His ability to take control of a situation was phenomenal, and it was mentally exhausting trying to keep one step ahead. We had discussed this topic at length with Jane, the psychologist, and developed strategies to try to prevent Wayne dictating our every move, but he could manipulate things at lightening speed.

One of Jane's suggestions was to give him two very clear choices, so we tried this one morning over the issue of getting up. Getting Wayne out of bed to get ready for school could easily become a battleground. Sometimes he would like Tim or me to lift him out; we saw this as part of the nurturing process he had missed out on, and we didn't have a problem with it.

'It is time to get up – will you get out of the bed by yourself or would you like Tim to lift you?'

'Tim can lift me…' Fantastic, we had given two clear choices and with no arguments a decision had been reached. But we should have held back with our self-congratulations – Wayne hadn't finished the sentence.

'…but not now. He can come back later when I am ready.'

Did you spot the loophole? We hadn't been clear enough with Wayne about *when* he needed to get up! We should have said something along the lines of:

'Unfortunately there is no choice about getting up; you have to get up *right now* to get ready for school, but you can choose how you are going to get up…' and then offered the choices. Having to think about every possible outcome for each instruction or request, and restructuring it to close all the possible "get outs" he could find, left us feeling like our brains had been scrambled by the end of the day.

'Tea is ready' just meant to Wayne that the tea was ready: it didn't mean that he needed to come and sit at the table. 'Please don't ride your bike in the road' had to become 'You need to stay on the pavement with your bike' or Wayne would fly into a rage, believing you were ending his playtime.

Ensuring that the bicycles were in good working order before the summer holidays so that Wayne and I could go out on them had been an unrealistic dream. He couldn't ride more than a few metres from the front door without overtaking me, standing up on the pedals and pedalling into the distance for all he was worth, regardless of the traffic or the terrain. Forever in my memory is the image of him as he left the path we were cycling along one day, totally ignoring my numerous requests to keep off the farmer's newly ploughed field. On he raced, clods of earth flying in all directions, before his bicycle ground to a halt, the wheels so caked with mud it was impossible for them to rotate. Wayne fell off the bike, jumped to his feet and turned towards me in angry desperation. My reaction was about as un-therapeutic as it could get – I dissolved into gales of laughter. The bicycle was wedged in an upright position, totally embedded in the mud and the only flesh visible when I looked at Wayne was a streak across his face where he had spread snot across it as he indignantly wiped his nose with his sleeve. Globules of mud hung from his hair and his frantic shuffling attempts to free the bike just made more and more mud cling to his shoes, which now resembled "moon boots". My laughter, as you would expect, did nothing to improve Wayne's mood. It also wasn't the response he was expecting. Wayne, in common with many children with attachment disorder, often created situations where he felt confident he would get told off, because that was better than the unknown – at least it was predictable! My laughter had clearly upset him.

'It's not f***ing funny, you stupid bitch.'

'I did ask you to stay on the path and not go on the field.'

'You didn't tell me it was f***ing muddy and that I would bust my bike.'

'It sounds like you think it is my fault.'

'Yeah, you never wanted to buy me a bike and now you've made me bust it. I hope you are happy now.'

'I am really sad that because you couldn't follow the rules and stay on the path your bike might be broken.'

'F*** you, bitch! You wanted me to break it; that's why you came here.'

This was another situation which could not be turned around so that Wayne would be able to accept responsibility for his actions. It was just too unbearable for him to do so, as it would reaffirm his core belief that he was bad – denial was the only option. At first we had found this difficult to deal with. 'It's sad that you can't tell me the truth about...' seemed much less effective to us than 'Go to your room and don't come out until you can tell the truth.' But on many occasions we discovered that what seemed like a bizarre solution recommended by Jane was, in fact, correct. Conventional parenting methods just didn't work with children like Wayne.

It was only a couple of weeks into the placement when my keys went missing. People who know me could be thinking 'What's new?', as my relationship with keys has never been good. If I added up the hours I have spent in my life looking for mislaid keys it would probably equate to months, if not years! It was no surprise that Tim's response, when I rang him at work to ask if he had seen my keys anywhere, had the tone of "Oh no, not again!" David and Malcolm reacted in much the same way, but I had searched in every conceivable and some less conceivable places and still there was no sign of them. My plans for the day had to be abandoned as the keyring held both my car and house keys. It was a little after lunchtime when the phone rang. It was the secretary from Wayne's school.

'I am sorry to trouble you, Mrs Miles, but we have just found a bunch of keys in Wayne's pocket and we wondered if they were from home or if they belonged to someone in school?' I should have felt relief that the keys had been found but instead I felt only furious about the amount of time I had wasted looking for them.

'They are mine – I've spent all morning looking for them.' As if it was her fault for not finding them in Wayne's pocket earlier!

'I will come and pick them up...no I won't, my car keys are on the ring, I can't get there.' I was being so bad tempered with the poor woman that she must have wished she hadn't rung me.

'I will give them to Wayne's taxi driver and he can give them to you when he drops Wayne off, unless you want to send someone to collect them,' she helpfully suggested.

Wayne would be home in a couple of hours so there was no point in sending anyone to collect them; it was too late to go out now anyway.

'That will be fine and by the way,' I begrudgingly added, 'thank you for ringing me.'

This type of misplaced irritation can easily become the norm if you don't keep a check on it. Children like Wayne can "wind you up" and in return they get understanding and empathy whilst others, often your nearest and dearest, have to face the consequences of their misdemeanours.

Once Wayne had returned home and I had been reunited with my keys, I asked him why he had taken them.

'I didn't; I found them at school and thought they looked like yours, so I picked them up and put them in my pocket for you.'

I had never heard anything quite so far fetched, so after attempting further discussion, with Wayne refusing to admit he had taken the keys, my patience ran out and I sent him to his room. I knew that there could be a number of reasons for Wayne's flat denial – fear of punishment, feeling a loss of control, a pattern of lying from the past that made it difficult now to tell truth from lies – and I remembered that Jane had stressed that trying to get a confession would be non-productive. But this was such an outrageous and obvious lie that surely even Jane would agree that I couldn't just let him get away with it. Sooner or later, wouldn't even Wayne see that this was just too far removed from the truth for me to be fooled? It was about 45 minutes later when Tim returned from work and Wayne was no closer to confessing. Looking back at it now, I can see how satisfying it must have been for Wayne to hear Tim and me debating the merits of sending him to his room. He was causing conflict between us and he thrived on conflict.

Tea was nearly ready and a confession was still not forthcoming, so I faced a dilemma: I couldn't deprive him of his meal, he had enough food issues already, but if I just called him for tea in the normal way then what sense did that make of sending him to his room in the first place? I had to face the fact that I had acted out of anger and frustration and not because I was thinking about what was best for Wayne. I had to do what I wanted Wayne to do…confess.

'Wayne, it's sad that you don't feel ready to tell me the truth about why you took the keys, but I can see that you are not ready to do that yet. I am sorry that I sent you to your room; it wasn't the right thing to do. I was cross about my keys going missing all day, and sometimes when we are cross we make mistakes and do the wrong thing and this was one of those times. I hope that one day you will be able to tell me the truth like I am telling you the truth now. It is tea time, so let's go downstairs, have our tea and we won't talk about the keys any more.'

Wayne remained silent but he joined us at the tea table, keys forgotten for that day at least. I had learned a really valuable lesson: with children like Wayne, you have to be more open and honest than you normally would be. I sometimes feel that I am wearing my heart on my sleeve where Wayne is concerned because letting him into my inner world is the only way he will start to understand his own feelings and make sense of them.

Over the following weeks and months, the disappearance of keys became a regular occurrence despite our attempts to keep them out of Wayne's reach. Whether he was inside the house or out, a key to either the front or back door seemed to be an important requisite for him – until all was revealed.

'Hi Wayne, good day at school?'

'Fine thanks…why are you always here when I get home?'

'What do you mean, why am I always here? I am here to look after you and keep you safe' (re-affirming that the adults in a child's life have a responsibility for keeping them safe is important). 'I like giving you a drink and something to eat and hearing about your day. That's what adults do, when they care about children.'

'So you won't lock me out and not let me in?'

'No – I will never do that. I am sorry to hear that has happened to you, but I promise that will never happen to you here. If I am not here, Tim, David or Malcolm will be and you will always be able to get in.'

'And out?'

'What do you mean... get out?'

Wayne looked exasperated. 'Will I always be able to get out too, you won't lock me in?'

'You've been locked in and you couldn't get out?'

'Yeah, Mum used to lock us in when she went out and if the electric ran out we had to wait in the dark...'

'That must have been really scary.'

'I wasn't scared but the little ones were. One day it thundered, then I was scared. I went under the table but I could still hear it and the others kept crying. It got on my nerves.'

I wanted to cry at the thought of five children, the eldest of whom couldn't have been more than six, in this situation. Trying not to show horror when Wayne shared these details about his previous life was one of the hardest aspects of caring for him. Any change in facial expression would cause him to clam up, engulfed in shame. It was often an internal battle for us, forcing our own feelings aside so that we could give him the support he needed, but also acknowledging our emotions so that we could explore them together later.

'I promise, Wayne, that you will never be locked in without an adult here. We lock the doors at night time to keep us all safe, but we will never lock you in on your own.'

Wayne carried on with the evening as if nothing had been said and he never took keys again. The keys had obviously been taken to ensure his own safety. What a huge amount of brain capacity he must have been using each day just to feel safe; it was no wonder that his academic progress at school was practically non-existent.

Meal times were one of the most difficult times of the day for Wayne, particularly our evening meal. Firstly, he really couldn't understand why we all sat around the table to eat and why we wanted to share our day with each other. One by one we would recount our news, ignoring Wayne's atrocious table manners, until eventually it was Wayne's turn. 'And how was your day, Wayne?'

'Why? What do you want to know for? I didn't do anything wrong, mind your own business.'

'We don't think you did anything wrong, it's just nice to find out what we have all been doing and talk about things. That's what families do, they share things.'

'I am eating my tea.'

'That's fine, you don't have to share your day if you don't want to, but we will ask again tomorrow just in case you change your mind.'

Secondly, memories of a time when there was no food meant that Wayne was on his guard throughout the meal, worried that we would steal the food from his plate. Sometimes he would wet or soil himself at the table in preference to risking a trip to the toilet and returning to find his food gone. Every day we told him that it was OK to go to the toilet if he needed to, no one would take his food, but he wasn't convinced. One day, David's girlfriend was going to stay for tea for the first time, so before the meal, I planned with her a conversation we would have at the table.

'This is your meal, Vicky, everything on the plate is yours and if you need to leave the table before you have finished, that is fine, no one will take your food.'

'Oh thanks, that's lovely, thank you for telling me it's all my food. It's the same in my house, but I know in some houses it's not like that, and people take your food if you go away from the table.'

'Shut up, shut up,' Wayne yelled. 'No one took my food when I left the table, that's lies.' We knew from Wayne's furious denial that we were on the right track but nevertheless we apologised for upsetting him. However, our reassurance that no one took food from other peoples' plates in our house clearly registered with him as he never wetted or soiled at the table again.

Buffet situations were a nightmare: Wayne would either cram his plate so high with food that it all fell off as he made his way back to his seat or he would stand as close to the buffet table as he could, just helping himself straight from serving plate to mouth whilst watching the remaining food like a hawk. He would pounce on any plates that looked like they would soon be empty, making sure he had his fair share of what was left. We worked with Jane to develop strategies to help Wayne cope with these situations – getting the food for him, letting him choose the food himself but only allowing him to choose a certain number of items, not allowing him to get to the table first – and they were all helping, but very slowly.

When you train a dog you are told that just because it will "sit" perfectly in your lounge, it won't automatically repeat the behaviour in a different setting and it will need to be retrained. In some respects this was true for Wayne. He found it impossible to adapt his newly-developing skills to different situations and we frequently overlooked this.

One Saturday evening, we made an impulse decision to eat in an "Eat as much as you like" Chinese buffet following a visit to a newly-opened cinema complex. We had enjoyed the film and the luscious array of food, tantalisingly displayed, and the low-cost "opening offers" lured us into the restaurant without a thought as to how Wayne would manage and what we would need to put in place to make this a successful evening. It wasn't until Wayne was making yet another visit to the buffet that the penny finally dropped for Tim. 'How many times has he been up there?' The consensus of opinion was that it was at least five, possibly six times; we were on our second helpings. When Wayne returned we suggested that he had eaten enough because he needed to leave room for his favourite part of the meal – the pudding.

'I'll just go once more and I will still have room for pudding,' he replied as he crammed his mouth with food at lightning speed.

By the time he was on his third pudding, we realised that by not taking control from the start, we had put ourselves in a position where it would be difficult to regain control without causing a major scene in the restaurant. What were we going to do? We started to make a plan as Wayne was filling his pudding bowl for the fourth time, but suddenly he dashed from the buffet to the table, banged down his bowl and ran to the exit. As I had been sitting nearest to the door, I was out of my seat and after him as fast as I could go through the crowded foyer. But there, lying flat on his back, right across the middle of the open doorway, was Wayne. People wanting to go in or out had to step over him. At first I thought he had slipped, but then I could see he was lying as straight as a rod with his hands by his sides.

'Wayne, will you get up please, people want to get past.'

'I can't – I feel sick.'

'Well, you have eaten quite a lot, but you don't have to lie there just because you feel sick. Get up and come back into the restaurant, then you can just sit quietly until we have paid and we can go home.'

'But they told me that if you lie down, you stop feeling sick and the room doesn't go round.'

'Is the room going round then?'

'No, but they said it would.'

I could only assume that he had been given these pearls of wisdom by someone in a drunken stupor. 'I think that is only if you have had too much beer to drink, and as you haven't had any beer, you don't need to lie there...get up please, because you are making it difficult for people to get past.'

'I've *got* to lie down.'

'What if you lie down in the car – will that be OK?' I hoped that by now Tim would have realised that we were not rejoining them in the restaurant and would come out to find us.

'Yeah, but I've got to lie down all the way home.'

Fortunately we have a "people carrier", so once the others had found us, we were able to head back to the car, change around the seats and let Wayne lie down all the way home!

Besides all the behaviours associated with lack of food in the past, food was also a great means of control for Wayne: he would eat his tea and declare the meal his absolute favourite but the next time you gave it to him he would gag as each mouthful passed his lips or point blank refuse to eat anything quite so disgusting. On one occasion, after huge protest he ate sausage, beans and jacket potato – another previous favourite – and had hardly swallowed the last mouthful before he deliberately vomited it back onto the plate.

He looked me straight in the eye and said, 'You didn't say I had to keep it down.' The rest of us were trying not to retch into our plates as well, but we knew that he was protesting at being taken away from the TV to sit and eat at the table, so I quickly moved my chair closer to him and put my arm around his shoulders. He jumped to his feet, declaring that he would go to his room as punishment.

'Wayne, you can't go to your room, you are sick, you need to stay close to me or Tim so that we can make sure you are OK.'

'No, no, I shouldn't have done that. I will go to my room.'

'But you are a sick boy and sick boys need to be looked after.' Glancing around the table, I asked the rest of the family what they thought. It was a unanimous decision: a very sick boy couldn't possibly go to his room alone – he needed continuous adult supervision to make sure that he was making a proper recovery.

'I am fine, I'm fine, that was stupid, I'm not ill really.'

'Sorry, but as we said sick children need to be carefully looked after, we couldn't possibly allow you to go to your room alone. That would be irresponsible of us. It's not a problem, we are happy to look after you.'

By bedtime Wayne was noticeably confused by our reaction: he had clearly used the tactic to take control of the situation as we had insisted that he join us at the table. In his world you didn't receive love and attention when you were ill, you were just left to get on with it or punished for making a mess. His strategy had backfired on him and there was no doubt in our mind that he would not repeat the behaviour again. But we could also see that he felt overwhelming shame that he had been so "stupid". This was another situation when arguing with him that he wasn't stupid would have only made things worse; again, empathy was required. Verbally expressing empathy was the easy part – getting the non-verbal communication right was more problematic.

So often in the busy lives we lead today, we are verbally communicating one thing while being distracted by another. Wayne needed our full and focused attention for however long it took. It would have been so much easier to have just told him not to worry about it and got on with our evening, but deep down we knew that wouldn't work. This model of care was far more demanding and intense than we had ever imagined. Had it really been developed to fit in with family life?

5

Finding the feelings

How on earth had he gone from playing on the floor with the toys in the therapy room to trying to escape through the open skylight?

Anne and I hung onto Wayne's legs and looked at each other in disbelief. Wayne had started therapy in the summer of 2005 and was having one fifty-minute session every week. Because of his dreadful nightmares about the past and his "Pandora's box" of trauma and attachment-linked behaviours, the therapy started earlier in the placement than had been originally planned. We hoped that giving Wayne a designated and safe space in which to explore the past might reduce the "acting out" during his day-to-day life. Anne, a therapist attached to the local specialist psychological support service for children in care and adopted children, facilitated the sessions but worked closely with Jane, the psychologist; with Wayne's permission, the sessions were also videoed. Jane and Anne were both supervised by Dan Hughes, whose model for family therapy we were following, and again, with Wayne's permission, the videos of the sessions were being shared with him.

At the first meeting Anne explained the "rules" to Wayne: the sessions would start and end on time; he would remain present in the therapy room for the designated period; and neither he, Anne nor I were to be hurt. We talked about confidentiality in the context of child protection issues. It was the first time I had attended therapy with a child in this way and I wasn't sure what to expect or how Wayne would react to my being there. I also didn't feel entirely comfortable with having my interactions with Wayne videoed and unpicked at a later date. I usually run at the sight of a camera; however, I could see the value of it and raised no objections.

The therapy room had the usual array of toys: play figures, animals, objects and symbols, glove puppets, dolls house and furniture, books, drawing materials, baby dolls and clothes, medical kit and building blocks. In addition, there were some more specialist "toys", including a set of masks showing different emotions and expressions, which Wayne was drawn to as he explored the room. He looked at them, shuffled them about, and then put them down and played with some of the other toys. As Anne continued to introduce the sessions, Wayne gravitated back to the masks. He stacked one on top of the other, placing the smiling happy face on top. Then he held the stack of masks in front of his face. It was incredible. What was Wayne showing us? A confusion of feelings with a beautiful smile on the surface! I knew at this point that our decision to start the therapy sooner than planned had been the right one.

On the way home from this initial meeting, Wayne asked if I could buy him a blanket to take to the sessions; he was very specific about the colour and texture of the blanket. Wayne's requirements didn't match current trends in the world of bedding and it was a real challenge to find exactly what he wanted, but having the blanket was clearly important to him. It became known as the "telling blanket" because Wayne could only tell Anne and me about the past if he was hiding under the safety of the blanket.

Before each session, Anne would ring me to discuss how things had been over the past week and identify areas to work on that day. The therapy started almost as soon as Anne met us in the waiting area to take us up to her room. What seemed to Wayne like general chatter as we climbed the stairs was, in fact, a carefully structured dialogue based on "Theraplay" techniques for children and their parents. The goal is to enhance attachment, self-esteem, trust in others and joyful engagement. Anne complimented Wayne on how good he was looking; how his jumper matched his lovely blue eyes; how beautifully long his legs were growing; how smart his new hair cut was. Every week she found something to enthuse over, and I added a few positive comments about Wayne at home. Once inside the therapy room, we noted the time and made sure Wayne knew where the hands on the clock would be when the session ended. The beginning and end of the sessions involved more play activities. Despite his age, Wayne enjoyed "nurturing" games like "Round and Round the Garden", "This Little Piggy" and "Mother Please May I?" and often asked for them at home when he was sure that neither David nor Malcolm were around to observe.

The middle section of the session focused on the treatment model we were using at home but with the emphasis shifting between the therapist–child relationship and the parent–child relationship. The "parent" in this situation becomes the co-therapist.

We recounted the successes since the last session; sometimes these were so small that in normal circumstances they wouldn't have been noticed: Wayne managed to stay at the table for the whole meal; he didn't make a fuss when it was bedtime; he managed to sleep in until 6am. Everything got a mention, in an effort to boost

Wayne's feelings of self-worth. Focusing on the successes of the week was also helpful to me as it was easy to get overwhelmed by the day-to-day, relentless hard work of caring for Wayne and the feeling that progress was non-existent.

Wayne's difficulty with trusting "parents" was explored both by discussion and by re-enacting how he would have been cared for if he had been with me since birth. I cradled, rocked and sang lullabies to him as we sat on floor cushions or the sofa in the therapy room. Wayne's long, gangly body spilled out of my arms, as he struggled to cope with this strange sensation. Anne would also ask me about difficulties Wayne had experienced since we last met; we were always careful to acknowledge how the past influenced Wayne's current behaviour, that he wasn't "bad", while making it clear that some behaviours were not acceptable.

Talking or even hearing about the past was incredibly painful for Wayne and would often trigger an uncontrollable rage. However, his attempted escape through the skylight was one of his more unpredictable reactions.

It was a hot summer's day about a year into the therapy, one of those familiar British summer days which are hot, humid and airless. Anne and I had been following the usual format of the sessions, when suddenly Wayne jumped up and, using the radiator as a stepping stone, proceeded to haul himself up to the open skylight, trying to push his head outside. We had no idea what had triggered this action – we hadn't been talking about anything particularly difficult. The room was incredibly warm and wrestling with Wayne was the last activity either Anne or I wanted to engage in. In polite society they say that 'ladies gently perspire', but there is no doubt about it – Anne and I were sweating profusely by the time Wayne was safely back on terra firma!

It was later that summer when Wayne had a major

outburst, refusing to get into our car, which was hot after being parked in the sun for some time, that I made the link. Wayne was being triggered back into trauma by warm enclosed environments as a result of being incarcerated in an under-stairs cupboard as punishment at a much younger age. In these situations, he always tried to get his head out of a window, assuming the door to be barred, hence his need to get to the skylight. Once his head was outside he would gasp at the air like a fish out of water until we could persuade him that the door was open and he could exit by a more conventional route.

What took place in the therapy room would often leave Wayne angry with his birth mother for the lack of care she had given him or with me for daring to suggest that her care had been inadequate. Either way, getting him home was often a challenge: Wayne saw me as the villain of the piece and the last thing he wanted to do was walk sensibly by my side back to the car. He became an expert at feigning a calm exterior before we left, but once outside the building he would hurl verbal and sometimes physical abuse at me and make off at speed, often threatening to run deliberately into the traffic. Once we were in the car his behaviour could make it unsafe for me to drive him home and I would have to send an SOS to our fostering service for support. Waiting for assistance to arrive seemed like an eternity and soon it was agreed that a social work assistant would collect me from home, collect Wayne from school, drop us both off for the therapy session and then wait to drive us back home. If it had been a particularly difficult session, and Wayne was still presenting challenging behaviour back at home, the social work assistant would stay until Tim returned from work. I found the sessions exhausting: keeping a close eye on Wayne's mood, noting his reactions to the different topics we discussed, following Anne's cues and being acutely aware of the fact that I was being videoed all took their toll, and a quiet lie down would have been preferable to an evening trying to contain Wayne's reaction to therapy.

To complement the more formal therapy sessions, helping Wayne to recognise and manage his feelings was an ongoing daily "drip, drip" process. We had realised early in the placement that the only emotions he knew about were fear and anger and we used every opportunity we could to make him aware of both his and others' feelings. We would watch films such as *Bambi*, *Black Beauty* and *The Railway Children*, describing either our own or the characters' emotions as the story unfolded. We knew we were making progress on the day he handed me the box of tissues, saying, 'The next bit always makes you sad,' as we watched *Black Beauty* for the umpteenth time.

We would also describe our feelings during day-to-day events, while listening to the news and in family discussions; we had never laid our souls so bare.

Trying to help Wayne explore his own emotions in relation to the loss of his family was more problematic. His three younger siblings, Lilly, Mark and Harry, had been adopted, and he only had annual "letterbox" contact with them. He saw his elder brother, Sam, who was fostered at the other end of the country, roughly every six weeks. This was usually in the school holidays, but their relationship was so destructive that visits had not only to be very closely supervised but also kept brief. His mother was unreliable and unpredictable; she often failed to turn up to the arranged contact or was unable to engage meaningfully with Wayne if she did. To Tim and me, it seemed counterproductive to make Wayne face up to his mother's inadequacies in therapy, but expect him to respond positively to her when they met. After a great deal of debate amongst Wayne's social work and therapeutic team, permission was sought and granted to suspend contact with his mother until he was further along in the therapeutic process.

Wayne loves the natural world, and we are indebted to the makers of the wonderful wildlife programmes shown on TV for the valuable resource they provided in helping us to help Wayne make sense of his family situation. One particularly useful series was the BBC's *Elephant Diaries*, which focused on a hospital and rehabilitation centre for orphaned elephants. The vulnerable baby elephants arrived at the centre traumatised, often malnourished and in poor health. Thanks to the devoted care and attention of the centre staff, the majority eventually returned to the wild, their mental and physical wounds healed. Wayne was able to tolerate us talking about how the baby elephants must be feeling, how dreadful it must be to lose your family, what a long time it would take before they would learn to trust the centre staff and how anxious and scared the baby elephants must have been when they arrived at the centre. There was an unspoken acknowledgement between Wayne and us about how the elephants' plight so closely mirrored his own. But talking about the elephants' feelings was so much easier than talking about himself.

Eighteen months into the placement, Meg, Wayne's social worker, arrived to see him for a routine visit. After the pleasantries had been exchanged and the customary cup of tea served, Meg edged excitedly forward on her seat, picked up her voluminous handbag from the floor and delved into its depths. After much rummaging around she triumphantly produced a brown envelope with all the aplomb of a magician producing a rabbit out of a hat!

'Wayne, this is so exciting! You have got a letter from Lilly and Mark.'

Wayne was sitting beside me on the sofa and I felt him stiffen at the mention of their names.

'Oh dear, Wayne, it seems like this is going to be "hard talking" for you to hear, what can I do to help you?' I interjected. I deliberately used the expression "hard talking" as it was something Anne and I used in the therapy sessions when we knew that what we were about to say would be difficult for Wayne to hear; we always made it clear how long we would talk about the subject for, and stop once the allotted time was up. I hoped that Meg would pick up on this expression and tone down her level of excitement. But no such luck.

She proceeded to read the letters word for word, totally oblivious to Wayne's growing inability to regulate his emotions. Lilly and Mark had been placed together and the letters had clearly been written by one of their adoptive parents. They listed their achievements, many of which exceeded Wayne's abilities despite them being younger. It wasn't until Wayne stood up, grabbed the coffee table and threw it from one end of the room to the other, then got on the window ledge and tried to climb out of the window, that Meg stopped.

I couldn't understand how Meg could arrive with the letter without checking out with us first how Wayne was feeling that day, how he was likely to react and the best way to approach the subject. I was furious. In fact, I could quite easily have poured the mug of tea I had just made her over her head, but instead I asked her less than politely to leave. That evening was hideous, with Wayne completely out of control, and it was several days before he began to stabilise again.

This wasn't the first time Meg had acted in a way that, in our opinion, ran counter to the aims of therapeutic fostering. One of our most significant previous clashes had been over Wayne's bike. The bicycle had survived its ordeal in the ploughed field, needing nothing more than a good wash down with the hosepipe. But Wayne had no concept of the need to treat it with respect if it was to remain his trusty steed: he rode it up and down kerbs at speed, did "wheelies" and other stunts on it and blamed the inferior quality of the machine when something broke and he was unable to ride it. It certainly wasn't his fault. When he needed his fourth replacement tyre in as many weeks we decided that using his bike without adult supervision was clearly a "no-no". We felt quite proud of the way we had handled the situation in true PACE style: taking responsibility by telling Wayne that allowing him to go out on his bike without adult supervision had been our mistake. We had asked him to do something he clearly wasn't ready for yet, and as a result he hadn't been able to keep the bike safe. In future he could only go on it if one of us was available either to go with him or to watch him. After initial protest Wayne agreed, and soon saw that his bike riding hadn't been curtailed too much, as we made sure that there was someone available when he wanted to play outside with his friends. I discussed what had happened with Anne and she thought we had handled the situation well. A couple of days later I relayed the tale to Meg in the context of 'Hey, at last I think we are getting the hang of this,' but was knocked backwards by her response:

'That's not acceptable – all children have a right to a bicycle, and you must give it back to him at once.'

'But we haven't taken it away, he can ride it when we can supervise him and someone is always here after school and at weekends.'

'But it is his bike and you can't take it away like that and he won't want you tagging along every time he goes out.'

'But surely that's what therapeutic fostering is all about – setting the child up to succeed? If we let him go out unsupervised, the bike will be broken, he will be plunged into shame and besides, we can't just keep paying out to get it repaired…are you going to pay for it?'

'You're just being facetious now, let him have the bike and go out with his mates like a "normal" lad.'

My temper was rising. Clearly Wayne wasn't a "normal" lad or he wouldn't have been referred to the therapeutic fostering scheme in the first place. Besides, Anne had said that what we had done was fine. 'Anne knows about this and she says we have done the right thing. I will get her to ring you…goodbye.'

I don't know what conversation took place between Anne and Meg on this subject, but Anne later confirmed that if high supervision levels enabled Wayne to achieve success it was the right thing to do.

Our next clash with Meg came over an invitation Wayne received to the birthday party of a child in his class. We knew that he would find it difficult to cope with the hustle, bustle and high excitement of a party. Excitement is as difficult an emotion to regulate as anger for children with Wayne's difficulties, but often people think that because something involves having fun, it will be fine. Meg clearly thought that. She was horrified when I told her that after discussion with Jane, we had arranged to arrive at the party halfway through. This would mean that Wayne could have some food, join in singing Happy Birthday to his friend, have a short time playing and then leave when everyone else did. Meg strongly felt that this would make Wayne look different; he would 'enjoy being part of the gang' and should attend the whole event. We argued that as we knew nothing about the family, or the level of supervision in place, our plan was preferable, but she was adamant. This posed something of a dilemma for us: based on our experience of Wayne and Jane's advice, we knew we should stick with our original decision, but should we overrule Wayne's social worker? After a lot of debate, Tim and I decided that as we were the people who would be picking up the pieces if things didn't go well for Wayne, we would go with what our instincts were telling us.

On the day we got our timing slightly askew and arrived at the party one-and-a-quarter hours before the end; we had intended to arrive a little later. As we lived some distance away, we asked the child's parents if we could stay – it was too far to drive home and then back again. Thank goodness we did! There were about 20 children of varying ages present and chaos reigned. The adults were doing nothing to supervise the proceedings, small "scraps" were breaking out and there was lots of rough and tumble. Wayne stayed welded to our side. We helped him choose his food, which he enjoyed. He then went to join some of the other children but kept to the sidelines, observing what was going on around him. Suddenly a girl of similar age ran up to him and slapped him on the face. He hit her back. Before we could intervene, the birthday child's granddad came into the hall; he was paralytic drunk and was lurching around the room. Wayne immediately ran and cowered behind Tim, hands over his head. Family members gathered around granddad; he was ushered out of the building, and Wayne came out of hiding. He stood silently watching for a moment or two before loudly announcing that if we didn't leave now he would miss his favourite TV programme. Wayne couldn't tell the time and had no idea what it was he wanted to watch when he got home, but we were elated. For the first time, albeit in a round-about way, he had been able to ask us to remove him from an uncomfortable situation. We were making progress.

We couldn't imagine what kind of state Wayne would have been in if we had followed Meg's wishes and just dropped him off at the party for the whole afternoon. It was becoming apparent that she didn't really agree with what we were doing. We were rapidly coming to the conclusion that people fell into four categories on the subject of this type of therapeutic care.

There were those who just didn't agree with it. On a foster carer training course, I heard one foster carer say to another, 'Have you heard about this therapeutic fostering scheme they've started? What a load of rubbish. These kids need a family, not a bloody therapist living with them!' 'Yes, it's ridiculous,' was the reply. 'If they ask me to do it I shall tell them what I think about it. Where is the love and care if you're giving them therapy all day? They just want to be like normal kids.' Other foster carers joined in the debate, and the unanimous conclusion was that therapeutic foster carers were cold-hearted, overpaid and probably just in it for the money. Several times I tried to interject to set the record straight. I could tell that they had conjured up an image of the child lying on a couch and the foster carers using some kind of psychological tricks to force him to change his wicked ways! As far as they were concerned, a strict set of rules, accepting no nonsense and a sprinkling of love could change everything. I have to confess that part of me enjoyed watching them squirm uncomfortably in their seats when they later asked me what I did.

There must be a second group of carers who can immediately see the potential of this way of working and have embraced it to the full.

The third group is made up of people like Tim and myself. We didn't fully understand the method initially, but we were excited by something new, curious and willing to "give it a go", and became total converts once we saw the changes it could bring about.

Finally comes the group which we believed Meg belonged to. She understood the theory but couldn't put it into practice, either because she felt a need to "compensate" Wayne for his previous life experiences, or because she saw it as cruel and punitive. We would have to agree that there is a fine line between being punitive and PACE methods, but the tone of voice, the ability to regulate your own emotions as a model for the child, and a sense of humour all put PACE and punishment worlds apart. There was no doubt in our minds that we were doing the right thing; we could see very subtle changes taking place in Wayne. But without Meg on board our progress was being held back. We always had a nagging anxiety that even though we knew we were making the right decisions for Wayne, Meg would overrule us and undermine Wayne's development. Having complained about Pam, Wayne's previous social worker, we were reluctant to do the same with Meg for fear of being branded "troublemakers". We were also acutely aware that being in contact with a severely deprived, neglected and traumatised child like Wayne can arouse feelings of anxiety, panic and despair – among other emotional states – in both individuals and institutions, and cause otherwise competent professionals to act out of character. We had chosen to take Wayne into our lives; the other people in his team had just acquired him as part of their caseload. However, we could see that we couldn't continue like this, and the way in which she handled the letters from Lilly and Mark was the final straw. Yet again, we had to make our dissatisfaction known, this time to Meg's manager, Linda. We couldn't help but wonder why the rest of Wayne's team didn't have to undergo the same assessment process with Jane as we did, in order to make sure that they too were up to the job!

It was decided that Joan would become Wayne's social worker. She was very experienced and had lived in the USA for several years so was familiar with Dan Hughes' methods. The relief we felt when we spoke to her about Wayne was enormous: she understood the behaviours we were talking about and could almost instantly give advice on strategies to manage them. She also seemed to be able to truly empathise with how it must feel to be caring for Wayne and the stresses and strains it put upon the family as a whole. At last we had a team that was working together and towards the same goal – helping Wayne to make sense of his feelings and to move on from the horrors of the past into what would hopefully be a brighter future.

6

Taking care of ourselves

Wayne seemed programmed to detect even the thought of any "hanky panky".

We knew that one of the main occupational hazards we faced in caring for Wayne was of developing secondary traumatic stress disorder (when carers develop the stress responses of the traumatised person they are caring for). Taking regular breaks is key to reducing the risks. Time off should include time for rest and relaxation, as well as the opportunity for pursuing interests and the more spiritual side of life.

But finding an outlet for the mixture of emotions we felt was not easy. The male members of the household all followed their outside interests and activities and Tim, of course, had his job, but for me it was more difficult. If Wayne was at school, and that was not always the case, it was fine: I could walk the dogs, fit in a session at the gym, a swim, an art class or meet up with friends. In the school holidays, or if Wayne was home for some other reason, by the time evening came I was too mentally exhausted to even contemplate going out. It wasn't a calculated decision but I found myself drifting back into a habit from my turbulent teenage years: keeping a journal. Usually I would take myself off to the bedroom after tea and just sit and write: sometimes it would be pages and pages, sometimes poetry and often just a string of words which, when I re-read them, made no sense at all. But if it had been a particularly challenging day, I would go as soon as Tim came in from work and "offload" into the pages of my notebook so that Tim wasn't deluged by my stress from the day, and we could chat about things more rationally later in the evening.

As time passed and the value of this activity as a release from the emotional impact of living with Wayne became more apparent, I indulged in more and more beautiful notebooks: gorgeous handmade paper, often embedded with dried flowers, rose petals and exotic perfumes; the covers depicting scenes of tranquillity, sometimes embellished with fine fabrics, "jewels" or pressed leaves. As Wayne shared more and more of his traumatic life experiences, the beauty of the book somehow diluted the awfulness of what we had to deal with day by day. I could close the pages and leave my emotions behind until either I had my consultations with Jane or Anne or discussed them with our supervising social worker, Rose, who had replaced Pam.

Elizabeth had filled the role of supervising social worker admirably between Pam's departure and Rose's arrival. We had ironed out most of the confusion and conflict between the various agencies which made up Wayne's team by convening monthly Core Group Meetings, which included Wayne's new social worker, Joan, and her manager who chaired the meetings, Jane, Anne, ourselves and of course Elizabeth, although Rose would now take her place. The meetings were used to discuss Wayne's progress and agree on appropriate strategies; it was beginning to feel like we really were working as a team.

Rose had been like a breath of fresh air when she breezed into our life in August 2005. She was similar in age to Tim and myself and had been a social worker for a number of years. She had also brought up four children of her own so she had a wealth of experience to draw upon. She was familiar with Dan Hughes' model of parenting and family therapy and had a very practical and realistic approach to supporting our work with Wayne. However, her best qualities were her honesty and fantastic communication skills. If she didn't know the answer to a question or how to deal with a behaviour problem, she would say so and together we would come up with a plan of action. Like all social workers, she had a busy schedule, but she always found time to respond to telephone calls and emails, even if it was just to say that she was busy and would contact me again to deal with the problem. This may seem a small detail but when you are working day and night in your own home with a traumatised child, you can quickly start to feel isolated, and even a brief contact to let you know that you are working as part of a team is very reassuring.

Getting a break from Wayne to allow Tim and myself to spend time as a couple was problematic. Our promised respite hadn't materialised, even though now that Rose was our support worker it was recognised by all that it was desperately needed. The problem was that Joy and Brian, the only respite carers with the relevant skills and understanding of the way in which we were working, were already committed to another child. To be fair to our fostering service, they tried to compensate us by giving us a small extra allowance for a regular babysitter. Sometimes we used this to pay Claire to take Wayne out so that we could catch up with things at home or just collapse in a chair with a cup of coffee. But the amount we were given didn't cover the cost of any activity, only Claire's time, so in order to get a decent break we were paying out a considerable sum for entertainment. We could, of course, just get Claire to babysit and go out for a meal or to the cinema, but often we were too exhausted to enjoy the evening and sat in the restaurant wishing we were at home. All we wanted was a quiet night in, time to relax and unwind, perhaps with a DVD and a glass of wine.

Our decision to put Wayne in the bedroom next to ours enabled us to react quickly to his night terrors and monitor if he was in or out of bed, but the downside was that he in turn could hear our every move. His hyper-vigilance and the fact that he was awake at all hours of the night put something of a damper on more intimate moments. Clearly, having been married for nearly thirty years and with both of us fast approaching fifty, we were not in the first stages of a passionate relationship, but more in what a friend once referred to as the "cosy, well-worn socks" stage! I am not sure if that was complimentary to her husband or not, but I knew what she meant: the stage when you are completely relaxed and comfortable with each other. However, she may have been on the right track with socks in our case, as Wayne's arrival had certainly caused an icy chill in our bedroom. At first we were so busy leaping in and out of bed all night in response to his nightmares or wet beds, so worn out by the non-stop mental stress of trying to keep one step ahead of him or by anxiously discussing how to deal with various problems he was presenting, that we didn't even notice that something was missing from our relationship. But once we became aware that, in what seemed like the distant past, things had been different, we found that trying to make more time for ourselves was hopeless. Wayne demanded our attention night and day and seemed programmed to detect even the thought of any "hanky panky", as he called it, and to cause a spectacular diversion!

Time dragged on and on and by the time Wayne returned to school after his first summer holidays with us, six months of caring for him without a break and the strain it was putting not only on our relationship but on us as a family was taking a serious toll. There was no way we could contemplate taking Wayne to Paris with us in October if we didn't get a break. I was so exhausted that I rang Elizabeth, Rose's manager, in tears. We were totally committed to Wayne but it was impossible to continue without a break. Luckily, my call to Elizabeth coincided with Joy and Brian becoming free to take Wayne. They had already been briefed and confirmed that they were willing to become Wayne's respite carers.

The moment I met Joy, I felt that we had known each other for years; we hit it off straight away. When Tim and Brian met, they got on well too, and we knew we had found the lifeline we so desperately needed. After introducing Wayne to Joy and Brian over Sunday afternoon tea, it was agreed that he would go and stay with them for a long weekend in a couple of weeks. Tim and I really couldn't afford to go away, with a family holiday booked for only a few weeks later, but we were so desperate for a break that we raided our "rainy day fund" and booked three nights in a hotel. We weren't sure how Wayne would react to this separation but Joy was full of helpful suggestions. We bought a few small toys and wrapped up one for each day we would be away. I found a small paper carrier bag and decorated it with pink and red tissue paper hearts and wrapped the handles with red ribbon. I tied a tag to each parcel saying something positive we would miss about Wayne: we will miss your beautiful blue eyes; your lovely smile that brightens our day...and packed the parcels in the bag, with a further tag on the handles: "Bag of Love". Wayne could open one gift each morning when we were away as a reminder that although he couldn't see us, we were thinking of him.

Joy and Brian had a veritable menagerie of animals, which was a big attraction for Wayne and he was looking forward to going to stay with them. We all set off in good spirits. Our break may have only been for four days, but to Tim and me it seemed like heaven: peace, tranquillity and time to be a couple.

Wayne too enjoyed his break, and spending one weekend a month with Joy and Brian soon became a regular part of his routine. One of the key things which made this relationship work so well for all of us was that Joy and Brian understood that the respite was for us and not an entertainment for Wayne. As far as possible they kept to his usual day-to-day routine. Of course, their interests and activities differed from ours, and this was great from Wayne's point of view because it gave him something different to look forward to, but it all happened within a structure that was familiar to him. They occasionally did something special like any family, but generally Wayne slotted into their normal weekend activities so that he built a relationship with them and not with the treats they offered. The other good thing was that they always gave us feedback on the weekend in front of Wayne so that there was no chance of "splitting" us.

Traumatised children are masters at splitting: playing one adult off against another so that rows and conflicts develop. It is another way in which they can feel in control. Splitting can happen between any of the adults in the child's life: between home and school, birth family and carers, social workers and carers, carers and respite carers and of course between the members of the foster family. By openly discussing how the weekend had gone, Joy and Brian immediately eliminated any chance of splitting. Wayne also knew that I rang Joy before he arrived at her house in his taxi from school to let her know how things had been with us.

Besides the lifeline Joy offered as a respite carer, she also became a close friend – one who truly understood what I meant if I said we were having a difficult time. Our other friends were great and gave us all the support they could, but they never quite realised the relentless nature of the difficulties Wayne presented. On many occasions when we would lament about a particular behaviour, they would respond with 'But all children do that.' Of course they do, but not with the frequency or at the same level of severity that Wayne did. As Joy and I discussed various aspects of Wayne's behaviour, it often put a new perspective on things, and our different interpretations of the same behaviour helped us to look out of the box and to try different ways of dealing with it. Joy and Brian were the only other people who lived with Wayne, and this gave them far greater insights than the rest of Wayne's team.

Our respite weekends started on Friday morning when Wayne left for school and ended on Sunday evening when Brian and Joy brought him back to us. At first it was difficult not to let Wayne dominate our thoughts and discussions throughout the weekend so that we ended up feeling just as we would have done if he had been with us! We tried to get into a routine of only allowing Wayne to "intrude" on Friday, reminding each other that the topic was off limits for the rest of the weekend.

We always made sure that we set aside one evening during these weekends to have a family meal at home with David and Malcolm. This gave us an opportunity to catch up with each others' news and for them to air any issues that living with Wayne had raised. We were acutely aware that Wayne's behaviour had ruined a number of family occasions for David and Malcolm. Striking the balance between letting Wayne know that we understood his behaviour, but that things would be better for us all if we could find ways to help him manage it more appropriately, was a continuous challenge, and David and Malcolm often had useful ideas about it.

This was also a time when David and Malcolm could invite friends or girlfriends home without risking that the visit would be ruined by Wayne. Seeing several young men in the house sent him back into a traumatised state. One evening a group of them were assembling at our home, ready for Tim to give them a lift into town for a night out. The usual lads' banter started to develop and one of them playfully poked Malcolm on the arm. Like greased lightning, Wayne was off the sofa, across the room and punching the "offender" hard on the shoulder, ready for a full-scale fight. He had no concept that this was just harmless fun and not a real threat to his or Malcolm's safety.

In the early days we were not able to use David and Malcolm as "babysitters" to give us a break because as soon as we were out of the door, Wayne would try to take liberties he wouldn't dream of taking with someone he knew less well. Out of the house this was less of a problem, and the twins played an important role in helping us preserve our sanity by taking Wayne to the cinema and bowling as well as shopping for music, video games and sometimes clothes.

Buying a summer house for the garden was another way of creating a sanctuary for family members: wicker chairs, lighting and an electric stove made it a cosy bolt-hole to escape to for brief respite, whatever the weather.

During school holidays, our fostering service runs a programme of activities for children approximately one day a week to provide breaks for their carers. Initially they were unable to offer the level of support Wayne required, so I went along on the first trip. Trying to manage his behaviour in a group of children from "difficult" backgrounds was a nightmare; it would have been far easier to have taken him out for the day on my own. I vowed there and then that I would never do it again: if there was no support for Wayne, he wouldn't go.

After about a year, Wayne had built up a really good relationship with the social work assistants and one of them would collect him from home and accompany him on the trips. Having one day a week in the holidays to catch up with household chores, get my hair cut or do something relaxing has certainly helped me survive the long summer holidays. Sadly, our ability to try and maintain our sanity was often hampered by what seemed like unnecessary battles with the authorities we were working with – usually over funding!

In addition to the standard fostering allowance for a child of Wayne's age, I am paid an enhanced fee to be at home full time in order to fulfil all the commitments that looking after Wayne entails: meetings, therapy, consultations and responding to any difficulties that may arise during the day. This probably sounds like a generous deal but it doesn't take into account all the extra costs associated with caring for a child like Wayne. You don't become a foster carer if you want to make money but you don't expect to subsidise the placement either. At the end of the first year of Wayne being with us, we calculated that we had subsidised the placement by about £4,000 to £5,000. The washing machine had been declared a "write-off" after dealing with up to three or four extra loads of Wayne's washing a day. Because of the extent of the bedwetting, Wayne's bottom was often sore and chafed. We provided disposable "night-time" pants similar to disposable nappies as well as absorbent pads so that he was never lying in a pool of urine. When I asked for extra funding to cover these items, I was told it was included in the fostering allowance.

Tim, who is self-employed, had taken time off work to attend training or be available for Wayne if I was on a training course. Our fostering service offered £3.50 an hour towards child care if we were attending training, but who on earth were we going to find to care for a child with Wayne's level of difficulty for that amount? So instead, Tim took the time off and had to pay someone to cover the work he should have been doing.

A support group was set up by Jane and Anne for the few of us involved in the therapeutic fostering scheme, which met monthly, and it was suggested that Tim and I should both attend. This, of course, would mean losing a day's earnings. We asked if our fostering service could reimburse him, and after much to-ing, fro-ing and negotiation, they agreed to pay only a percentage of his loss of income for the day because 'he was asking for rather a lot'. In fact, he was only asking the standard self-employed builder's rate for our area. Clearly, he wasn't as valuable an asset to the service as we had thought! For much of the first three years Wayne was with us, the placement would not have survived if it hadn't been for Tim's willingness to support me.

One area that the scheme appeared to have overlooked was support for Wayne to join in social activities, such as cubs, football, cricket clubs and the like. It was difficult for Wayne to take part without additional support, and of course he often didn't want me tagging along if other children's parents weren't there. He was particularly keen to join a local children's art group, which met after school in the local community centre. The group was privately run and cost £7 for the two-hour session; Wayne would need someone to take him and stay with him and he was adamant that it wasn't to be me. At first I asked if a social work assistant could do this but that wasn't possible and I was told to find someone myself. Claire offered to take it on but, of course, would charge us her usual £7 per hour. Our request for funding was turned down, so the cost to us was £21 per week, which had to be added to the cost of all other social activities we paid for.

Wayne's sporting skills were way below those of his peers, which made it almost impossible for him to join in without having his self-confidence undermined further. He gave the local under-11s football team a go but quickly stopped being picked for the team when he scored in whichever goal was closest to him, and the team was rapidly losing its place at the top of the league table. So we started to encourage him to take part in individual sports where he could work at his own pace. Wayne was keen to learn to swim but his school refused to take him swimming because of health and safety reasons. We could see their point, but we felt strongly it was important that he learned to swim, not only for the sense of achievement but because it could save his life.

We discovered that our local sports centre offered one-to-one lessons for children with "special needs" at a cost of £15 per lesson, and we again asked for a contribution from our fostering service. We were turned down point blank and told to enrol him for the cheaper group lessons. We were determined not to be beaten on this: surely they could see that Wayne would be unable to wait his turn in a group of 15 or 20 children and would start jostling or just take off into the pool without regard for his or anyone else's safety. He needed one-to-one attention to keep him engaged throughout the session. I carefully prepared a written risk assessment detailing why it wasn't a feasible option for him to join the group lessons. Eventually it was agreed that I could claim the cost of the lessons back on a monthly basis. Wayne took to the lessons like a fish to water and very quickly gained his distance and water skills badges; it was clear that it was an area in which he could excel. But instead of feeling triumphant, we felt disheartened that we had to jump through hoops in order to get Wayne the level of support he required. Over the following years, we would discover that this was nothing, and that we would have to go way beyond what should be expected of foster carers in order to secure Wayne the services he needed.

Holidays were a bone of contention, as taking Wayne away was certainly no holiday for us. Allowing ourselves to be pushed by Pam into taking Wayne on the trip to Paris is something we now regret. We don't blame Wayne in any way, just ourselves for not fighting harder to get Wayne into respite care for the duration of the trip. We had prepared him as best we could, taking him to the airport a few weeks before our departure to watch the planes taking off and landing and to see the various procedures we would go through. We shared books on Paris and watched videos on Disneyland, but still he was in panic mode.

I fly because it gets me from A to B, not because I enjoy it, and I often suffer from motion sickness, so feel quite anxious myself until we arrive at our destination. Wayne's running commentary throughout the flight on the number of plane crashes he could recall, both fact and fiction, did nothing to calm my nerves. Much to the amusement of our fellow travellers as we landed at Charles de Gaulle airport, Wayne let out a loud expletive '...Well that was a waste of time, we're back where we started!'

It wasn't until we were well out of the airport that he noticed we were driving on the 'wrong side of the road', which confirmed that we were indeed in another country! Throughout our stay, Wayne kept yelling out the names of the makes and models of the cars we saw. Here we were in one of the most beautiful cities in the world and all he could do was yell out 'Ford Fiesta, Vauxhall Corsa...' Months later we realised that he was creating a sense of safety by focusing on the familiar. His high-pitched and disparaging remarks about the Mona Lisa seemed to echo round the Louvre and we hoped and prayed that there were few English speakers present. We had to agree that this work of art was very much smaller than we had imagined, but there was no need to be quite so rude about it.

However, our time in Disneyland was by far the worst part of the trip. Wayne refused to queue: either he would try and barge to the front, regardless of the fact that I had his pass and he could go nowhere without it, or he would sit on the ground and refuse to move with the queue. Often, after the ordeal of the queues, he would take one look at the ride and refuse to get on it, forcing Tim or me to miss out on it too. By our last night his behaviour was "off the wall" and in the early hours of the morning Tim and I were sitting out of his earshot, one on the toilet and one on the edge of the bath in the hotel, wondering how on earth we were going to get him on the plane to go home. We were so cross that we had felt forced into bringing him, and about the huge disappointment the trip had been for Malcolm and David, that we seriously considered ringing our fostering service and asking them to send someone to collect Wayne. A trip like this was something we would probably never do again with David and Malcolm now that they were 21; it had cost what to us was a huge amount of money, which we felt had been completely wasted, and as a family we were barely speaking to each other. Our trip back to the airport was somewhat subdued and Wayne must have picked up that our patience was nearly worn out, as he barely spoke a word until we were back home.

This dreadful experience made us realise that taking Wayne out of his familiar environment raised his anxiety levels and his need to be in control so much that any future breaks with him would have to be entirely Wayne-focused. The route would have to be precisely planned to ensure that he was satisfied that there would be sufficient toilet stops. Each day, activities would have to be planned according to how he was managing his emotions. We became first class at on-the-spot risk assessments, as Wayne's reactions to new situations were never as expected. But this again raised the problem of cost. Like most foster families, we received an annual holiday allowance for Wayne, but taking him away was more stressful than caring for him at home, so we had to have a separate holiday to recover, when Wayne would go to Joy and Brian for a week. This allowed us to explore further afield and to pamper ourselves a little, but it also doubled our holiday costs and Tim had to take double the time off work! Our fostering service suggested that rather than taking Wayne away, perhaps we should just do day trips. But how would Wayne learn to cope with things if he didn't experience them, and Tim would still have to take the extra time off work. It was another hidden cost that our family budget would have to absorb.

As I recall these situations in order to record them here, I am transported back to feeling like the whingeing old hag I felt like on many occasions as I battled to resolve these issues. It drained me of some of the emotional energy I needed to care for Wayne, and took up time I should have been using to look after myself in order to be strong enough to meet Wayne's needs. Without Tim's dedication to our work, we would have been unable to continue, yet he has had to make huge sacrifices, both personally and financially. If Tim had been employed he would probably have been sacked by now: he has taken so much time off or has had to rush home to help me keep Wayne safe. Without Tim's support, we would have been forced to let Wayne go to a residential setting for the rest of his life – something the scheme had been set up to avoid. These unnecessary battles leave you feeling worn out and demoralised, especially when so often they are with the very organisations that supposedly are working towards the same goal as you are! When we started this journey we were determined not to become cynical, like so many of the people we had met in our years of fostering, but slowly we edged down that slope and hung on by our fingertips, hoping we wouldn't fall off the edge.

7

Education, education, education

We were prepared to go to the top to make sure Wayne's case was heard.

Tears streamed down my face as I trudged slowly back up the hill, my dogs faithfully by my side. Given that they knew that at any moment they would be clipped back on to their leads, our morning walk nearly at an end, this was unusual. It was the weekend: David and Malcolm were at home looking after Wayne, and walking the dogs had given me time to ponder our desperate situation. It was April 2007 and Wayne had been out of school or only receiving a few hours of formal education a week since January. How had things gone so badly wrong for Wayne, and, more to the point, how could we find the strength to continue? I was mentally exhausted from caring for Wayne 24 hours a day as well as having to produce a satisfactory home teaching timetable, often without input from the education department. We had also been besieged by family problems.

As I passed through the gate, which separates the open countryside from the village, I glanced into the window of a friend's house. She often displays greetings cards she has received and particularly likes, but today instead, she was prominently displaying a card with the following verse:

Don't quit

When things go wrong, as they sometimes will
When the road you're trudging seems all uphill,
When the funds are low and the debts are high
And you want to smile, but can only sigh,
When care is pressing you down a bit,
Rest if you want, but don't you quit.

Don't give up, though the pace seems slow,
You may succeed with another blow.
Success is failure turned inside out
– The silver tint of the clouds of doubt.
And you never know just how close you are.
It may be near when it seems so far.

So stick to the fight when you're hardest hit.
It's when things go wrong that you mustn't quit.

– Author unknown

It was as if she had put it there for me, yet she knew nothing of my state of mind. Yes, the going was tough but around the next corner could be the solution; I somehow had to find the inner strength to keep going.

Over the next few days I reflected on Wayne's educational history. He had missed most of the "early years" experiences and as far as I could tell didn't have the foundation skills he needed to build on. His behavioural difficulties had always overshadowed the academic side of school life, and sadly he had therefore spent more time out of school than in.

His time at the Behavioural Unit when he was placed with us had given him his first positive experience of education. Mr Page, who ran the unit, was working in a way that complemented what we were doing at home. The tightly-structured programme created a safe and secure environment. During breaks the children didn't join the rest of the school in the playground; they had their own "garden" just outside the unit where they spent time creating a haven for squirrels, a variety of birds and wild flowers. The area flourished under the children's care and also provided live entertainment as the children set up a number of challenges for the squirrels to reach their food. The children didn't miss out on the rough and tumble of the playground as they had supervised playtime after the rest of the school went back to their classrooms. Playground "marshals" organised games like hopscotch, skipping and rounders, so that the children were able to develop their physical and social skills in a protected environment.

Wayne found both literacy and numeracy hard. He was way behind his peers but had no inclination to make progress as he could see no purpose in it. From a very young age he had "wheeled and dealed" and had got hold of enough money or goods to survive. He knew the street value of a variety of easily obtainable automobilia, such as wheel trims and car badges, and told of a scam he and his brother, Sam, had run: taking newspapers out of people's letterboxes, replacing them with old copies and then selling the current ones on the street. Who needed to be able to read or write?

After sixteen months under Mr Page's care, Wayne started to flourish. Then came the bombshell: his behaviour had improved so much that it was no longer justified for him to take up a place in the unit, which was for children *with* behaviour problems. Much to our astonishment and despite warnings from Wayne's "team" of the possible consequences, at the annual review of Wayne's Statement of Special Educational Needs (SEN) it was decided that he no longer had behavioural problems!

The SEN review didn't take place until mid-June, so there was little time to plan his move to a new school, but because of his poor literacy and numeracy skills he was allocated a place at a nearby school for children with learning difficulties for the following September. The arrangements were made in such a rush that there were only two half-day preparatory visits. Vital information about Wayne was not given to the new school, so there was no time to make their usual in-depth assessment. At the age of ten-and-a-half, Wayne went from the nurturing environment of the unit, which had a ratio of one staff member to two or three children, to a class where no designated teaching assistant support was provided.

The impact on Wayne was enormous, and within weeks the supposedly "cured" behavioural problems had re-emerged, and by the end of the autumn term exclusions were becoming an almost daily occurrence.

'Mrs Miles, can you please come into school – Wayne is on the school roof...on the roof of the minibus...has poured paint all over the classroom floor...smashed a window.' I often didn't agree with Wayne being sent home for these misdemeanours; I felt it would be much better for him to make amends for his actions, and indeed Dan Hughes places a lot of emphasis on consequences: 'Consequences with empathy ensure that the parent does not reinforce her child's behaviour through a negative emotional response to it' (2006).

On the day Wayne squirted all the bottles of poster paint he could find onto the classroom floor, much to the Head's despair, I refused to take him home until he had been on his hands and knees with a bucket of water and a cloth and cleaned it all up. Sending him home seemed to me the easy option and was probably what he wanted as he clearly wasn't coping in the school, and in our opinion he was being re-traumatised. Whilst I had empathy for how dreadful he must be feeling, he had to learn that the solution wouldn't come from manipulating the school staff into giving in to him.

'Wow, Wayne, you have made a real mess here, I am guessing that inside your head it feels like a big mess too, with everything mixing up together like the colours of the paint. Look, here is a big dark area of paint, that is going to be hard to sort out and I think the school mess is going to be hard to sort out too…' Bucket after bucket of dirty water flowed down the sink and slowly the tiled floor started to reappear. Finally we had finished.

'There you go, we got there in the end, the mess has all gone. When we get home we need to talk about the mess in your head because we can sort that out too.'

We knew that legally Wayne had to attend school but each day it was getting harder and harder to send him. As I put him into his taxi each morning, I knew that within a short space of time I would be jumping into the car, having been summoned to collect him. I carefully recorded every incident and relayed in meetings our concerns about the psychological damage we believed was being done to Wayne. But despite sympathetic noises from Wayne's "team" and the school going through the motions of trying to resolve things, nothing changed and we were left under no illusion as to what the consequences would be if we failed to ensure that Wayne attended school.

Because of the various difficulties of the children in Wayne's class, the environment was chaotic and unpredictable. One girl had Tourette's syndrome and shouted out expletives every few minutes, one lad refused to use the classroom door and would only enter or exit through the window! Without a designated one-to-one teaching assistant to help him understand the nature of the other children's difficulties, Wayne was in "fight or flight" mode. Jane had made several visits to the school to give them strategies to use to help him, but I suspected that Wayne's teacher had no time for these "new-fangled" methods and just continued in her usual way. At first, his worsening behaviour was confined to school, but as the term drew to an end towards Christmas, it had spilled over into our home – in fact, things had become so bad that it wasn't safe for me to be at home alone with him. Tim was having to finish work early to be home when Wayne returned from school, to be on stand-by at work ready to dash home if Wayne was excluded and he also took a much longer than usual Christmas break. This had a huge physical and emotional effect on us as a family, not to mention the knock-on effect on our finances.

As Wayne's behaviour was so unpredictable and violent at times, making him a danger to himself and others, Tim and I were trained in "safe holding techniques", all of which required two people. If the techniques were used, we had to provide a written report within 24 hours of the incident, which was circulated via email to all of Wayne's "team". Jane or Anne and Rose were always quick to respond, but Wayne's social worker, Joan, seemed not to remember that she was supposed to make a home visit within 24 hours of being notified. She would often attend meetings and appear to have no idea about the difficult behaviours we had been dealing with. Pressure of work resulted in her being out of touch. Having to sit in a meeting recounting events which I had stayed up until one or two in the morning to record was frustrating in the extreme. I often left these meetings in tears.

Tim and I were also concerned that whilst we had received appropriate training, we had nothing in writing to confirm that there might be times when we would need to "hold" Wayne. We were worried what the consequences would be if something went wrong. It had been agreed in a Core Group meeting that a written Behaviour Management Plan was required, but meetings came and went and no plan materialised. We felt vulnerable and exposed; the situation demanded that "holding" continue and we just hoped for the best.

We thought that the Christmas break would give Wayne time to stabilise before the new term, but this wasn't to be. If for any reason Tim couldn't be around, the difficulties would escalate. Wayne was only willing to co-operate in activities of his choosing and became aggressive and confrontational if he couldn't get his own way, saying that he would "do me" if I didn't give in. He frequently threw things at me and hit me as well as being verbally abusive. On one occasion he tried to pin me to the wall and write on my face with a felt-tip pen, yelling 'The sight of your ugly face makes me sick!' If I tried to move to another part of the house, he would follow, taunting and poking me. He would lie in wait if I needed to go to the toilet and then pounce on me and try to knock me to the floor as I came out.

Malcolm nearly lost his Christmas job at a store in the city as a result of Wayne refusing to get ready in the mornings so that I could drive Malcolm to catch the Park and Ride bus service. Jane suggested we devise a consequence for Wayne's behaviour, but what consequence could we impose to make him get out of the house in time for Malcolm to catch the bus, and how could Wayne compensate him if he lost his job? Joan suggested that I shouldn't be giving him a lift anyway; he could get a taxi... at a cost of £20 each way!

Christmas was all but written off: Tim's elderly parents usually joined us for lunch on Christmas Day but Tim arranged for his sister to go to their house and cook instead. If it hadn't been for David and Malcolm, we would have cancelled it altogether! By the time Wayne returned to school at the beginning of January, we were more physically and mentally tired than we had ever been. Tim hastily arranged to take the first week of term off so that we could try and recover while Wayne was at school. But no such luck – within an hour of being on the premises Wayne had smashed the glass in a door and been excluded.

The following week I attended a meeting, which had been arranged sometime earlier, with a heavy heart. After much soul searching we had decided, as a family, that either Wayne had to be removed from school while they sorted out more support for him or we would have to end the placement.

It was agreed that a one-to-one teaching assistant would be recruited to support Wayne full time in the classroom and playground and to help him make sense of what was going on around him. With Jane supporting our request, it was agreed that Wayne would be educated at home until this person was in post.

As soon as we told Wayne that he wouldn't be going back to school until he had a designated person to support him, he started to calm down. After a week of low-key activities and reassurance that when he returned to school he would be safe, we felt able to start introducing some school work. The home tutors for our area had not had their contracts renewed by the local education authority, so there was no one available to help us. The school sent work and I sat with Wayne and did my best to "teach" him.

One of the conditions attached to allowing Wayne to be removed from school was that I produced a written weekly timetable covering normal school hours. Because we were working at home with fewer distractions than in the classroom, and because we were working more intensively, the work the school sent home only covered a fraction of the week, so I had to develop my own curriculum. Walking the dogs became nature studies and numeracy; we took the wildlife identification book with us and "spotted" birds, butterflies, trees and insects. We measured the depth of the water in the stream and kept charts and graphs. An outdoor thermometer recorded the daily temperature, which again we transferred to charts and graphs. A fading flower border was dug up and replanted as a wildlife area. Swimming became PE and the local museums and art galleries were a regular destination.

Time passed, and despite various attempts, and hours and hours spent in meetings to discuss a reintegration plan for Wayne, a teaching assistant with the level of experience needed to support him hadn't been found. Jane felt that the physical environment of the school was also a contributing factor to Wayne's inability to cope. The school was moving to new purpose-built premises in September, so it was decided to delay Wayne's return until the new school opened.

What had started as a brief intervention to stabilise Wayne and save his placement with us was now putting the placement at risk. Apart from a few hours a week, which Wayne was spending with two behavioural support workers to prepare him for his transition back into school in September, he was at home with me full-time. The school was no longer sending work home, so I had to devise more and more educational activities.

Tim was at home too, having not worked for nearly four months. A niggling back pain in early January had worsened and transpired to be three prolapsed discs. He was waiting to go into hospital for surgery and in the meantime could only get around by using two sticks. Sadly, Tim's dad had recently died and Tim felt he was letting his mum down as he was unable to give her the support she needed because he was doing the best he could to help me with Wayne's home education. Having Tim out of action felt like having one of my limbs amputated as it completely turned upside-down all our routines, roles and responsibilities. The wonderful respite Joy and Brian had provided for nearly two years was also coming to an end. They had decided to move into providing full-time therapeutic care, and there was no one to replace them.

Everyone in Wayne's "team" was sympathetic to our plight and as frustrated as we were, but apart from some funding towards a cleaner, no practical help was forthcoming. A support worker had initially taken Wayne out a couple of times a week, but he had left to move on to pastures new, and the local authority, in their wisdom, had frozen recruitment, so he had not been replaced. Serious "cracks" were starting to appear in Wayne's team as conflict arose between the various agencies and us about the type of education Wayne required, who would provide it and, more importantly, fund it.

My usual strategies for maintaining my sanity had been erased by our circumstances, and my consultations with Jane and Anne, which were another way to offload, had practically ground to a halt as there was no one to care for Wayne while I was out. Although Tim was at home, his state of health wouldn't allow him to take sole charge of Wayne without risking further injury to his back. It seemed that as the going got tougher the network supporting the placement was falling apart. We were repeatedly being pushed to breaking point: surely anyone could see that we couldn't go on like this. The fact that we were so close to the placement breaking down was unbearable. We had spent over two years doing everything we could to enable Wayne to form an attachment to us and that had been impossible to do without forming an attachment to him. Now it looked as if our family would be torn apart and the pain would be as great as losing David or Malcolm. But we just couldn't go on. When Tim came out of hospital he would need help with washing, dressing and the like – how was I supposed to manage that and educate Wayne? Wouldn't it be nice if just for once our fostering service asked what they could do to help? Tim suspected that they hadn't asked because staffing cuts meant that there was nothing they could offer. This may have been true but it would have been far better to acknowledge it than take the ostrich approach by burying their heads in the sand. Not for the first time, I found myself on the phone in tears to Elizabeth, begging for support.

Eventually a plan was put in place for Wayne to spend some of his "school" hours with another foster family who were currently without a placement. After some initial hiccups over transport, the arrangement worked well and I suspect that Wayne was as pleased to have a break from us as we were to have one from him!

By July the new school was nearing completion and we were invited to go and look around. I was particularly keen to see the room Wayne could go to with a teaching assistant, either to "cool down" if he was angry or to work one–to–one. I imagined a space similar to the Chill Zone at the Behavioural Unit but I couldn't have been more wrong. I have seen bigger broom cupboards. This was a small, enclosed space, with no windows and barely room for a desk, let alone any cushions or other furnishings to make it a cosy safe haven. I pointed out the problems Wayne had with small, enclosed spaces, but was reassured that by September all would be well.

September saw Tim return to work and Wayne eagerly set off to rejoin school life. This was initially for mornings only, supported by the two behavioural support workers, as a suitable teaching assistant had still not been found for the salary on offer. I heaved a sigh of relief as his taxi pulled away on the first day of term; I had been hanging on by the skin of my teeth and needed to give myself some serious TLC. But my "pampering" was short-lived. Two days into the new term, I was summoned to the school because Wayne was completely out of control. It sounded serious, so I contacted Joan in case I needed support to get Wayne home. She agreed to meet me at the school; I jumped into the car and dashed off, unknowingly collecting a speeding ticket en route.

I could hear Wayne yelling as I walked down the corridor towards his classroom but couldn't believe what I was seeing. Two, by now exhausted, members of staff were hanging onto the door handle of what I continued to refer to as the "broom cupboard", keeping the door closed to stop Wayne escaping. I could see through the small pane of glass in the door that Wayne's face was bright red; he was frantic and sweating profusely. I asked the staff to let go of the door as calmly as I could and I went in to Wayne. He was worn out and in fear of his life. There were footprints from the soles of his trainers where he had literally climbed the wall trying to escape, and some of the ceiling tiles lay shredded on the floor as he had punched through them to see if he could escape through the roof. He must have been terrified. The staff lamented the damage Wayne had done to their lovely new school and Joan, his social worker, was nowhere to be seen; she had decided to wait in the office to see if I really needed her before setting off.

I left the door open and sat in the "broom cupboard" with Wayne. We were both crying. I had become the rescuer in what is sometimes know as the "Drama Triangle" that children like Wayne create: he was the victim and the school the persecutor. I just wanted to scoop him into my arms and take him far, far away to a place where he would never be treated like this again.

Over the following weeks it became apparent that having Wayne at home for nine months so that everything he needed at school could be put in place had been a complete waste of time: the educational provision he needed and what the local education authority were able or willing to offer were poles apart. The final straw was when his amended Statement of Special Educational Needs, which had mysteriously been delayed in the system, plopped through the letterbox. It bore no resemblance to the Draft Statement we had approved; much of the provision Wayne needed had been deleted. When I queried this with the local education authority, they said the school couldn't make the provision identified so it had been removed. I saw red: if that was the case, then clearly he was in the wrong school. We had nothing to lose now. We couldn't continue with the current situation so we had to start making the local education authority realise that we wouldn't allow Wayne's placement to break down over education issues without a fight, and we were prepared to go to the top to make sure Wayne's case was heard.

By November, we had very reluctantly agreed for Wayne to go on a trial of the Attention Deficit Hyperactivity Disorder (ADHD) drug, Concerta. There is so much controversy over the use of these drugs that we had always vehemently refused any suggestion that Wayne should try them. But we felt we had to give his current school one last shot, and this drug just might help. The medication had a major effect on Wayne and I found myself having to eat humble pie – he was so much calmer and able to think before he acted – but the school reported no difference. We couldn't help but wonder if they had seen a way to move Wayne on and were not going to back down now.

Then came a glimmer of hope. One of Tim's nieces sends her children to a Rudolf Steiner school, and she told us about an Independent Special Needs school, The Castle, which is based on Steiner principles. She felt sure it was just right for Wayne and it was within reasonable travelling distance. Tim and I agreed that we wouldn't follow procedures to get the local education authority to check it out; we would do it ourselves and tell them if we thought it was suitable.

We instantly knew that this was the place for Wayne, when we stepped from the car and were wrapped in a blanket of peace, tranquillity and warmth. The school was set in extensive grounds with an abundance of wildlife; it had a spiritual quality that was difficult to describe but somehow made you feel whole. The staff were amazing and instantly had a good understanding of Wayne's needs; the classes were very small and there was a wealth of practical activities on the curriculum, which we knew Wayne would excel at. Our next job was to convince Wayne's "team" and the local education authority that this was the right place for Wayne – and get them to agree to fund it.

By January 2008, Wayne had visited the school and given it his seal of approval. Having met and assessed him, the school was happy to offer him a place. But despite a consensus from all concerned that this was the best school for Wayne, the funding was not forthcoming.

Wayne was attending his current school for only two hours a day. The behavioural support assistants who had been working with him in the classroom had been withdrawn with little notice, and the school could not provide more support from their existing resources. If staff were off sick or not in school for any other reason, he was not allowed to attend. By now, he had more or less been out of education for a year. Our family, friends and even casual acquaintances were appalled that a child in the care system was being failed so badly. We were receiving advice from all directions, including details of a London solicitor who fights for education issues for children in care. I contacted him and gave him an overview of the case. He was willing to act on Wayne's behalf and highlighted a number of ways in which Wayne had been discriminated against and in which the local education authority had acted illegally. We had three options: we could meet with him in London, let him review the file, and he would then notify the local education authority of his intention to take legal action against them. For this he would charge £500. Or we could provide him with Wayne's details – so far we had kept his identity confidential – and he would apply for Legal Aid for Wayne in his own right. He would then fight the case with no charge to us. Or we could simply inform the local authority of our intention to take legal action in the hope that this might give them the push they needed.

We couldn't sleep, Tim couldn't eat, and I was eating too much! We were in total despair – this wasn't what we had signed up to when we took Wayne into our lives. No education, no respite (despite every effort, no one had been found to replace Brian and Joy), and a team with heavy workloads and torn loyalties – wanting to support us on a personal level but having to act professionally on the basis of available resources.

The piece of prose that had been sent to us just before Wayne's arrival was proving to apply to us as much as it did to Wayne. Tim and I felt like we were on a sinking island and at this point it was only our growing love for Wayne that was preventing us from going down and giving up on the placement.

We decided that we would make one last attempt to get funding for the Steiner school, and if that failed we would instruct the solicitor to act on our behalf. We couldn't really afford £500 but we wanted to feel we had done everything we could to secure Wayne the education he deserved and we didn't want to look back and feel we had failed him too. We informed our fostering service of our intention to take legal action; we also sent a letter stating our case to the Director of Children's Services. Within 24 hours we had verbal agreement for funding and formal agreement followed soon after.

As the Steiner school didn't follow the national curriculum, the next step was to get approval from the Department for Children, Schools and Families. Eventually approval was verbally agreed and it was decided that Wayne would leave his current school in February half-term and start at his new school after the holiday. Finally, hope was very firmly on the horizon.

8

Unmentionable behaviours

**I found myself making sure my cleavage was
well covered up.**

If there is one thing we have learnt from our years of
fostering, it is that some behaviours children display are
unmentionable. They are skirted over, rephrased or
diluted in reports and often not even discussed between
social workers and foster carers. If these behaviours are
not addressed, they can have far-reaching, lifelong
consequences, yet information or training to deal with
them is hard to find.

The paperwork we received about Wayne prior to his
arrival with us stated that he had been seen 'playing
inappropriately with dolls', but what did that mean? He
shouldn't have been playing with them because he was a
boy? He was being too rough? We suspected it meant he
was playing in a sexualised way, but no one offered any
details.

Within days of Wayne's arrival with us, we could tell that
he had more sexual knowledge than most lads of his age.

Our first trip out as a "family" was to the cinema and as we pulled into the car park Wayne wound down the window and called out 'All right love...nice tits!' Wayne had leaned across Malcolm to make this observation but had then ducked down leaving Malcolm exposed as the guilty party. Scantily clad females on the television or billboards received similar attention, as did David's and Malcolm's female friends.

Wayne was sitting on the sofa watching television one day when Tammy called for Malcolm, who was still grooming himself in front of the bathroom mirror. So Tammy joined us in the lounge.

'Sit down, Tammy,' Tim said. 'Wayne, move up so that Tammy can sit down, you don't need the whole sofa.' Wayne huffed but moved up.

We chatted for a while and then I noticed that Tammy was edging further away from Wayne – his hand was on her inner thigh and travelling upwards. This wasn't the only occasion when girls were treated in this way. If they arrived in short skirts or with bare midriffs, Wayne's excitement levels would rise and he would need continuous reminders of how to behave. One of David's girlfriends, on her first visit to the house, was greeted by Wayne in the hallway with a cheery enquiry into whether she and David had "shagged" yet.

But one of the worst incidents of a sexual nature was triggered by Wayne attending a Personal Health and Hygiene talk at school, without our knowledge, when he was ten years old. It was a Monday evening and Tim was, as usual, at choir practice. Wayne was afraid of the dark, so at bedtime I accompanied him upstairs. I waited outside his room while he got ready for bed and then he called me to say goodnight. As I entered the room, he stood on his bed in front of me with his pyjama trousers pulled down, and he started to pull his penis with one hand and point with the other, saying 'Look, look, I'm growing hairs, that means I can make a baby.' I said that I thought he was a bit young for making babies but he told me that a lady had come to school that day to show a film and talk about growing up.

I had no idea what the content of the film had been. I guessed it was about puberty, but it had clearly triggered memories of sexual scenes Wayne had either witnessed at first hand or seen on videos or DVDs. He was now recounting his observations in graphic detail and was clearly feeling aroused. I tried to calm him down by reminding him about different relationships – particularly those between mums and sons – but he was so "high" he was unable to hear me. Suddenly Wayne leapt off the bed, knocking me to the floor. I lay flat on my back knowing that if I didn't get up quickly I could be in trouble. By the time I got to my feet Wayne had wrapped a cord around his neck, tugging at it as he shouted 'Stupid, stupid, that's what I am, stupid.'

Trying to take the cord away would only have resulted in a power struggle and fuelled his determination.

'You are not stupid, you just got confused and over-excited. I am going to ring my sister and ask her to come and make us a nice cup of tea.' Thankfully, my sister was home and able to come round and stay with me until Tim returned.

Wayne was lying in his bed awake when Tim got back, probably expecting to be told off. Instead, Tim went up and said, 'Bad day, don't worry, we will sort it, we will get through it together.' We could have sat up with Wayne talking all night but it would have achieved nothing, he had no idea why he had behaved as he did.

The next morning I rang the school. Despite being aware of Wayne's troubled history, they had no concept of how he might have been affected by the lesson, and saw no reason why we should have been warned in advance that it was due to take place.

Tim's choir night became an evening when Wayne would "act out". Was this because Tim's absence triggered memories of "Mum at home alone", or was he consciously choosing to act out in a sexualised way when I was on my own? We never found out.

It was a Monday night again when Wayne hauled out the dressing up box and started to rummage around. He found a pair of high-heeled shoes, a skirt and a long blonde wig. 'I am Judith,' he announced, as he paraded around the lounge. He spent the evening wearing the clothes but he had dressed up before so I wasn't concerned.

At bedtime he insisted on keeping the wig on and sat in bed preening himself. As I went to leave the bedroom having said goodnight, he got out of bed and laid on his side on top of the quilt, with his head propped on one hand, legs slightly apart and pouting seductively. I ignored the behaviour and went out of the room saying I would be back up in half an hour to put his light out. Wayne jumped up, pulled his pyjama trousers down and knelt on the edge of the bed pushing his bottom at me.

'Wayne, it's time for bed now.'

'Go on then, go on.'

'I think you have got confused. I think you are asking me to do something that adults shouldn't do to children. I am really sad if that has happened to you before but it won't happen here.'

'What is it, then, that I want you to do?'

'Well, it has obviously got something to do with your bottom...'

'Like what? Disgusting things or would you like to spank me?'

'You know we don't hit children in this house and we don't do "disgusting" things either. I want you to know that it's not your fault if something "disgusting" has happened to you. A little boy can't stop adults doing things like that.'

Wayne turned and started hitting me, he grabbed my

arm and twisted it round. 'Do you want it f***ing broken, because that's what you'll get...bitch.'

I kept asking him to let go and calm down but he refused. He had a really tight grip on my arm. Suddenly he said: 'I'm f***ing out of here and going home.' He made a dash for the stairs.

By now I was getting used to these Monday night outbursts and had my mobile phone programmed with my neighbour's number in my pocket. Before Wayne could get out of the door she had arrived and Wayne stopped in his tracks. He went off to bed without a fuss. After a few minutes I went up to check he was OK. He had moved his pillows to the foot of the bed and had put his alarm clock and bedside lamp on the bed where he should have had his head. I acknowledged that perhaps he needed to sleep upside down tonight, and it was OK to keep the alarm clock in the bed, but I pointed out that it was too dangerous to have an electric lamp in the bed so it would have to go back where it belonged. As I bent down to pick it up he tried to punch me in the side of the head. I had anticipated this and managed to move out of the way. At this point, David and his girlfriend came home and came upstairs to say "hello". Wayne started chatting to them as if nothing had happened and then settled down to sleep.

I was worried that my physical appearance was exacerbating Wayne's difficulties. I have more than my fair share in the chest department! I found myself making sure my cleavage was well covered up, particularly if I was likely to be crawling around on the floor playing with him. If Wayne wanted a cuddle I made him sit by my side and I put an arm around his shoulders and strategically placed a large cushion over my chest and shoulder for his head to rest on.

I was often alarmed at how strongly I reacted to these sexualised incidents; my gut reaction was horror. We all know that these things can happen to children, but having scenes acted out that suggest that it may have happened to a child you care about is unbearable. I had heard that some carers feel aroused by it; I felt physically sick. As soon as I could after these incidents I poured my feelings into my notebook, often shedding tears when I thought of Wayne's lost innocence. With my writing I tried to cleanse my mind of the images Wayne had created.

Snow

Snow falls gently and silently
Cocooning the earth
The soft white fleece settles
The earth looks cleansed...pure

Each flake has a role to play
Softly nestling against its neighbour
Creating a protective blanket
Until new life can begin

Our love is your snow
Flakes so small they seem insignificant
Its touch so gentle...imperceptible
But slowly you will feel its caress

Spring brings forth buds fresh and new
Tender shoots reach out
Nurtured by the sun's gentle rays
Pale and unblemished delicate blossoms
Burst forth heralding a new beginning

Our love will be your springtime
In its warmth buds of hope slowly unfurl
A metamorphosis begins.

We had no idea if Wayne had been sexually abused himself, or had been subjected to watching sexual acts or pornography, but getting appropriate books on the subject was difficult. I often had to import them from the USA or Australia and without the internet would have remained ignorant. I felt that here in the UK we were still in denial about the sexual abuse of children.

I knew we couldn't change the past. Wayne had been robbed of his childhood and nothing could change that, but I hoped that each incident he acted out was a step closer to healing and having a future to look forward to.

The second unmentionable behaviour is self-injury, which was hinted at by the head teacher when I met her prior to Wayne moving in with us, but this was quickly smoothed over by his social worker. We had never cared for a child who self-injured before, so the first time Wayne grabbed a pencil off the coffee table when he didn't like something we said and started to stab himself in the throat with it, we were completely taken aback. The more we tried to stop him, the more determined he became. He then held the pencil at each end and pushed it down on his adam's apple.

'You do realise that could kill you?'

'I don't care, I'll stab myself in the back, then you will be happy.' He moved the pencil to the base of his spine and banged himself against the wall to try and make it pierce his back. Of course, the pencil broke. Pencils were one of his favourite weapons. They were easy to get hold of and had a convenient point. He would often return from school with his trousers stuck to dried blood where he had surreptitiously gouged his leg with a pencil without being noticed. Any scrape or scab offered an easy access point, and so minor injuries had to be bandaged out of all proportion to their size. Trouser legs and jumper sleeves provided tools for attempted self-strangulation if he wasn't getting his own way.

We had received no training on dealing with self-injury, but our gut instinct was that there were two sides to this behaviour: on the one hand, we felt that it was a kind of self-punishment as once, after gouging his leg until a steady flow of blood appeared, he cried, 'If only I had looked after them (*siblings*) better, we might still be together.' He believed he deserved to be punished for his failure to keep the family together. But on the other hand, we felt it was a learned behaviour to gain our attention. We suspected that he had observed his mother self-injuring and saw it as a tactic for coping with stress or taking control. But we were nervous about making a wrong decision and having something dreadful happen. I spoke to the community paediatrician and described Wayne's self-harming. She felt he wasn't at high risk of strangling himself with sleeves and trouser legs. But we were still anxious about taking a laid-back attitude in case things went wrong. I repeatedly asked my fostering service if they could find a course for me to learn more about strategies to use, but they could not find one.

As time passed we became better able to distinguish between serious signals of distress and attempts to get his own way, so that we stopped rushing to him like bees swarming to a honey pot. It was a risky course to take, and not one we would recommend, but thankfully it worked: the self-harming drastically reduced.

A less unmentionable behaviour, but nonetheless difficult to deal with, was what we called Wayne's "toilet troubles". When he came to us, he was soiling and wetting both during the day and at night. He was often totally oblivious that an "accident" had occurred, which left him vulnerable to bullying and ridicule both at school and socially. We knew that as a toddler he had lived in various "squats" without a proper toilet. Previous carers had reported that he urinated in any room of the house and over clothes and toys. We decided to go back to basics with the implementation of a "toilet training" plan, which we backed up by sharing the child-friendly leaflets that the organisation ERIC (Education and Resources for Improving Childhood Continence) had supplied. Wayne was amazed to learn that he could control his bladder – the first time I asked him to try and stop his urine in mid-flow he looked at me as if I were crazy. Within three months of being with us, the soiling had ceased completely and only night-time wetting remained. What surprised us was that Wayne had clearly never been toilet-trained before. We can only guess that each previous carer had assumed someone else had tried it.

One of the early indicators that Wayne was being re-traumatised by his school was that he was to-ing and fro-ing from the classroom to the toilet repeatedly. This then became a problem at home, before spilling into all areas of his and our life! It became impossible for him to leave the house without repeated visits to the toilet. On one occasion he went thirty times before being able to walk the family dogs. Car journeys became a nightmare, he jumped out of the car in order to urinate in some very dangerous places, opening the window and reaching out to over-ride the child locks.

Once when we stopped at a set of traffic lights, he got out because he saw a café on the other side of the road and knew they would have a toilet. We had only been underway for twenty minutes. On another occasion, he jumped out into the bushes while we were in a traffic queue – as you would have predicted, the traffic moved off at that point. We had some very frustrated drivers behind us as we tried to persuade him to get back into the car.

We could probably write a book on the toilet facilities of the Scottish Highlands – Wayne visited them all when we were there on holiday. In fact, once we found a toilet he would run in and out of it repeatedly, forcing out the very last tiny drop of urine. However, even this was preferable to him refusing to leave the accommodation because he didn't know where the toilets would be! Any attempts we made to delay urination resulted in a toddler-style tantrum.

After nine months of this behaviour, Wayne himself was getting upset by the situation. He said, 'I want to stop now but my brain won't let me.' The behaviour had clearly become an obsession. We knew that young people who haven't developed secure attachment patterns often use an addiction or obsession to replace the inadequate attachment figure. The ritual and routine Wayne initially used to create a sense of safety had now become a dependency without which he was unable to function. It was also clear that at the time he lacked the skills to express his emotions and communicate how he was feeling. We could identify a number of reasons why the behaviour had started – the question was, how did we make it stop?

Wayne had other "obsessional" tendencies. He would find a new hobby or interest and would only be able to talk about that, regardless of the situation. You could be trying to find out what he would like in his sandwich and he would be telling you in detail about the latest hub caps on his favourite make of car!

I scoured the internet: there was lots of information about obsessive behaviour, but no guidance. Anne was on maternity leave and my consultations with Jane were mainly focused on the pressing issue of school.

I consulted the community paediatrician who took time and trouble over the problem, drawing diagrams for Wayne of his internal workings. He said he understood but he still couldn't stop. Next she suggested using a timer, and asked Wayne to wait one minute, then two, and gradually build up the time after he asked to go, but he became hysterical. I read as much as I could on the subject of obsessive behaviours and then came up with my own plan. I bought some "child friendly" books on the subject to help Wayne understand the problem; these were fantastic and really helped him to see what was going on and to reassure him that he wasn't alone. We bought a plastic "urinal bottle" from the chemist to take when we went out, and also gave Wayne the option of wearing a pair of absorbent pants intended for night-time use. He felt that the bottle and the pants were too embarrassing and that he would just tell his brain to stop lying and reassure himself that he could wait.

We also helped Wayne to control the behaviour by telling him to go to the toilet frequently; that way, he could say that he didn't need to go, rather than listen to his internal voice, which was in overdrive. If we were intending to go anywhere, we would plan the trip, clearly identifying toilet stops on the map or making a list: park car, go to toilet in M&S, go to WH Smith, back to M&S for toilet, and so on. Once Wayne could "see" the frequency of his "visits", he could also see how big the problem was, and this helped him to have the resolve to overcome it. Finally, I used balloons and jugs of water to demonstrate how much his bladder could expand, and to assure him that there was no need to worry about having an "accident".

The fact that Wayne was out of school meant that the various elements of the plan could be incorporated throughout the day, rather than a specific time being set aside for the work. This helped it to be diluted in terms of it not being seen as a huge problem that needed therapy. The fact that Wayne himself realised that it was an obsession and that he needed help contributed hugely to the success of the intervention. Neither Wayne nor I commented as the behaviour slowly reduced and we were able to start going about our days in a more normal way. I was worried that mentioning it might trigger things off again and I guess Wayne was too. It wasn't until months after he had started at the Castle School that he said, 'I am so pleased that I don't have to keep going to the toilet now.' I made an exaggerated expression of great relief, hugged him and told him that I was really pleased too. Wayne smiled and nuzzled his head into my shoulder; another step along the road of trust had been made.

9

Grief and loss

We made small cardboard "coffins" lined with tissue paper.

'How long is a funeral?' Wayne asked, peering at the clock.

'About half an hour to an hour,' I said. 'Why?'

'They seem to have been gone a long time.'

The "they" he was referring to were Tim, David and Malcolm, who were attending the funeral of a young man, Chris, who had lived in the village. He was a little older than David and Malcolm and had been killed in a tragic farming accident. I had been unable to go to the funeral as it was an extended half-term for Wayne, who was waiting to start at his new school.

'The funeral will be over by now, but after the funeral you usually go back to the family's house or to the pub or a café and have a drink or a cup of tea and remember all the happy times you had with the person who has died. I expect that is where they are now.'

Wayne looked thoughtful for a moment, then, head down so I couldn't see his face, he said, 'No one made me a cup of tea when Lilly, Mark and Harry were taken away and I felt like they died.'

I felt a physical pain in my chest as he spoke; it was the first time he had been able to speak about this loss or even acknowledge that it had happened without flying into an uncontrollable rage. I took his hand and looked at him. 'I am sorry that no one did that for you...would you like a cup of tea now?'

'No thanks, I'm OK.' His face said, 'It's nice of you to offer but it's a bit late now.'

'I can see that it must have felt like they died. You didn't know where they had gone nor if you would ever see them again and no one helped you to understand, did they?'

A rare moment of silence followed. Wayne put his head on my shoulder and guided my hand to his head: one of the comforting things he liked most was for me to gently wind his hair round and round my finger.

'You will see them, one day. When you are a man you can look for them.'

Wayne gazed at me but said nothing; the subject was closed for that day.

Trying to help Wayne understand grief and loss had been incredibly difficult. The wildlife programmes helped, but Wayne remained detached and didn't use the chance to explore his own emotions. The first real opportunity presented itself when Dic and Dom, the goldfish, died. Wayne had enjoyed watching them swim around the tank as he lay in bed at night, and the fact that they contracted some kind of fungal infection and died almost at the same time was something of a double blow. We decided that one way to help Wayne with his feelings about the loss was to have a funeral. We planned it to be in the back garden where other family pets had found their final resting place under a tree. But Wayne had other ideas. He was adamant that Dic and Dom were to be buried in the front garden, as close to the pond as possible in case they wanted a swim!

We made small cardboard coffins lined with tissue paper. Wayne decorated them with fishy scenes and the ceremony began. Much to David and Malcolm's embarrassment, they were required to attend the "service" in full view of all our neighbours. We thanked Dic and Dom for the pleasure they had brought, their beautiful golden scales, the way they came up to the top of the tank for their food as soon as the lid was lifted. Then came the hard part as we remembered other special people and pets that were no longer with us – not only those who had died, but those who, for whatever reason, we no longer saw. Wayne didn't join in as we named the people we were thinking of, but we hoped something might be stirring inside him.

Wayne had locked his siblings away in his memory just as they were on the day he saw them last. Time had passed but as far as he was concerned they remained the same. "Letterbox" letters would arrive with photos showing them as they were now, but Wayne couldn't comprehend these changes.

He would have no involvement himself in the letterbox scheme. I would read out what I had written but he would cover his ears, turn up the TV or sing – he wanted no part of it.

Of course our "drip, drip" approach used every opportunity to weave the theme of loss and the associated emotions into our lives. Tim's parents were quite elderly and had been married for over fifty years when his mum needed a long hospital stay following a fall. His dad struggled to cope and couldn't contemplate a life without her. He refused to visit her in hospital, claiming that, if for any reason she didn't come home, he wanted to remember her as she was. Despite the fact that he regularly saw her apply colour to her almost white hair, he fondly said to Tim, 'Ahh...your mother's a marvellous woman and her hair is as black today as the day I met her; there's not many women you can say that about.'

Wayne started to correct him '...but I've seen...' Tim held a finger to his lips and shook his head. 'Don't, Wayne, we'll talk about it later.' This provided an excellent trigger to talk about the truth sometimes being too painful to discuss.

Some months later it was Tim's dad, not his mum, who passed away. Tim comes from a large family and both his parents thrived on visits from their grandchildren and great-grandchildren. When Wayne joined us he was treated just like the rest and welcomed into the bosom of the family. He in turn became very fond of them and enjoyed seeing them. When he heard that "Grampy" had passed away, he had no idea how to react. A large smile spread across his face but he clearly knew that it was inappropriate as he covered his mouth with his hand. He knew he needed to say something but clearly didn't know what.

'Wayne's really sorry to hear that your dad died,' I suggested.

'Yeah, I was sorry to hear about that, I liked him, and he was kind to me. I know he made me tired because he was hard to talk to with all that shouting I had to do, but I feel sad because I think I will miss him.'

Wayne quickly got the hang of modelling his own reactions to situations on ours; we weren't sure that he understood, but it helped him to behave in a more appropriate way. We gave him the option of coming to "Grampy's" funeral, but he decided against it and, being out of school, went to other foster carers for the day. When he came home, he asked how things had gone, but before Tim could reply he suddenly said, 'Did you ride in a limo?' Tim said that we had. 'Wow, was it exciting? Were the seats made of leather? Did it have black glass?'

'Wayne, I am just wondering if you think Tim might have been too sad about his dad dying to be interested in the car and what it was like. What do you think?'

'Yeah, sorry about that, I didn't know.' And truly he

didn't. He had been cut off from his own inner life for so long that we wondered if he would ever reconnect with the most painful parts of it.

But there were signs that we were making progress. He managed to choose the photographs to include in the letterbox letter that year and to write his name as best he could at the bottom. Following the incident with Meg and the letter, I had requested that the letterbox contributions were sent to me and I would share them with Wayne when he was having a good day emotionally. It was a Saturday morning when the letters from his siblings arrived. Wayne was in good spirits and he was still in bed practising being a teenager – although becoming one was another year away! I took them upstairs and quietly said, 'Wayne, your letters from Lilly, Mark and Harry have arrived. Shall I read them to you?' Wayne nodded and patted the bed, indicating that he wanted me to sit on the edge and read them. Whilst I read each of the letters, Wayne studied the accompanying photographs silently. One by one he stood the photos on the cupboard beside the bed.

'You can keep the letters but I will have these.' He dived under the bed and rummaged around in a box for a while before producing the only photo he has of his mum. It is a dreadful photo, blurred and overexposed. He placed it face down besides those of his siblings, before thinking the better of it, and roughly returning it to the box.

Over the next two months, the photos remained by his bed and we would casually make observations about similarities between Wayne and his siblings and how hard it must have been when they were separated. But there was no comment from Wayne until the day he made the connection between the young man's funeral and his own feelings of grief. It had taken three years to achieve this. Rewards like this might seem small but to us they were huge and oh-so-sweet.

Wayne's older bother, Sam, was in a therapeutic

fostering placement at the other end of the country. The boys had such a difficult relationship that it would have been impossible for them to live under the same roof without risking their emotional and physical wellbeing. As the two eldest, the boys had often been left in charge of their younger siblings at an age when they could have hardly looked after themselves. As a result, they developed a "dog eat dog" relationship where their own survival was paramount. At first it seemed like a huge effort to travel so far for contact, which often couldn't last for more than an hour, but the key thing was to make it a positive experience.

As time went on, and the boys made individual progress, their relationship started to improve and we could extend the time they spent together. Then, very slowly, they started to discuss snippets from the past and acknowledge that the reality was that neither of them was to blame: they had been given too much responsibility at too young an age. Sam had a close relationship with his mother prior to being taken into care. He had the benefit of being the only child until Wayne came along, and this resulted in him being very protective of her. Wayne, on the other hand, fluctuated between being fiercely protective and not even wanting to know she existed. Her photo was frequently moved between his bedside and the box under the bed. If I did something Wayne didn't think was fair, he would get the photo out and position it so that it was looking at me when I walked into his room as if to say, 'You're not my mum!' Sometimes he would sleep with it on or under his pillow; at other times he would try to throw it away. He was working out: who is this person and how does she fit into my life? The decision to suspend contact with her while Wayne was receiving therapy wasn't taken lightly but we felt he needed time to reflect on the past and come to terms with it. He seemed much calmer once the decision had been made and the anxiety of would she or wouldn't she turn up had been removed.

After about a year Wayne started to be aware of the difference between the care he was getting from us, and what she had given him. He was able to speak in a very mature way about her inability to meet his needs and look after him. He accepted that he could not live with her again. One day he had a fall from a friend's trampoline and hurt his neck. As we returned from the hospital, he said, 'Thank you for taking me, I'm not worried about it now because I know it's not serious. My mum wouldn't have taken me, she would have ignored me and I would have gone on being scared.'

Later, Wayne's understanding turned to anger: 'Don't talk to me about that f***ing bitch, she's not my mum, she didn't look after me right.'

'But you have to understand she had lots of problems…'

'What, like drugs…?'

'Sometimes drugs…'

'Yeah…well, she's not mine.'

From quite a young age, David and Malcolm had a very positive understanding of the circumstances that led to them being removed from their mother's care and adopted. We hoped that they could help Wayne to make sense of his story.

Sadly, Wayne's world remains either black or white and there is still much work to be done.

10

Good times

'What's the point?' he replied, 'You will be selling them soon anyway.'

'I have had such a nice time, I am going to scream,' Wayne announced as we left the tiny hall in a nearby village. We had been to my aunt's eightieth birthday party, so it had hardly been every twelve-year-old's dream night out, but Wayne really had enjoyed himself. The buffet had consisted of all the traditional favourites: crisps, sausage rolls, sausages on sticks and best of all, as far as Wayne was concerned, sherry trifle – not just any old trifle, but one with sherry, which made it "grown up".

The entertainment had been a local folk group singing familiar songs with which even Wayne joined in. But the high point of the evening, in Wayne's eyes, had been an elderly friend of my aunt who nodded off with her mouth open after one sherry too many. Her false teeth danced in and out of her mouth as her head dropped forward and jerked again as she drifted in and out of sleep. Finally, she fell into a deep sleep and her mouth opened further, sending her false teeth clattering to the floor! Wayne laughed so much he cried – and we cried watching him – we couldn't believe that this was the same boy who had arrived with us three years earlier unable to believe he deserved fun of any kind.

'Wayne, if you seriously are going to scream, can you please wait until we are in the car,' Tim requested, 'we don't want to disturb the neighbours.'

The doors of the car had barely closed before Wayne let out an ear-piercing scream. 'Thanks, Dad,' David and Malcolm chorused.

'I am so happy, I am going to scream and scream,' Wayne informed us as another ear-splitting sound reverberated around the car.

Tim started the engine; he clearly planned to get us home as fast as he could.

Once we were inside the house, Wayne started to chant, 'I've had a lovely time and I am not going to spoil it,' over and over again.

'Well, sadly, all lovely evenings have to come to an end,' I cautiously told him, waiting for the protest to start. But true to his word, Wayne got ready for bed and settled down without incident and with a beaming smile on his face.

Tim, David, Malcolm and I could hardly believe it. A "good time" of any sort usually triggered an outburst of some kind from Wayne before the day ended. We all hastily prepared for bed, keen to ensure that there was no activity in the house to disturb Wayne and break this magical spell!

As had often been the case since Wayne joined our family, Tim and I lay wide awake in the darkness, talking in whispers.

'We've done it, can you believe it?'

'Sshh, don't say that or we'll wake him up and he'll have a wobbly.'

'Yes, but we have, this is the first time we've done something special and he hasn't had to spoil it.'

We lay in silence, reflecting on our achievement.

Then we began to reminisce: 'That first holiday we took Wayne on. Can you remember how he kept getting in and out of bed all night to check that the sea was still there? Then the next morning he went for a swim and drank the water; he came running up the beach, gagging on the salt, but before I could get the orange squash out of the bag, he put his head into a rock pool, and drank that, not realising it was sea water too!'

'...And what about David and Malcolm's birthday holiday in Paris? That was a nightmare! I was so cross that we'd spent all that money on a holiday, and he ruined it.'

'Can you remember the night when he kicked you and chanted, 'You are not my mum, you are not my mum, get off me, get off me,' all the way from Disneyland back to our hotel? We spent all night locked in the bathroom, so he wouldn't hear us planning how we were going to get him back on the plane the next morning.'

One by one, we recalled the times when what should have been fun, enjoyable or a celebration, had been ruined by Wayne's overwhelming need to destroy the "good times". His core belief – "I am bad" – had convinced him that he didn't deserve anything "good" and he would go to extraordinary lengths to prove it.

The first birthday he spent with us was, on Jane's advice, very low key. I invited my nephew and niece, who are very close in age to Wayne. My sister didn't present it as a party to her children, she just said that they were bringing Wayne his present, so that they could leave easily if Wayne found it difficult to cope. We played Pass the Parcel, Hunt the Treasure and some games from a helpful publication called *Self-Esteem Games* by Barbara Sher (1998). The "party" went well, but Jane had warned us that Wayne would sabotage the day before going to bed. He broke some of his gifts; posted some CDs he had been given down the side of his cabin bed and generally did everything he thought would get him into trouble. Tim and I fixed a smile on our faces and overcame each obstacle as it arose: we mended toys, retrieved the CDs and commented on how lucky it was that none of the things flying around the living room had broken anything or hit us or the dogs. Wayne wouldn't give up, and continued to try to rile us until 11pm when he collapsed and went to sleep. The next day started badly, but we pointed out that nothing he did would spoil the lovely time he had on his birthday, and eventually he calmed down.

The following year we got more ambitious and allowed Wayne to choose a friend to take to see a show at the local children's theatre, followed by a rare visit to McDonalds. Again, the celebration went well, but again Wayne had to try and spoil the end of the day with appalling behaviour.

By the third year, Wayne decided to opt out of anything other than a family celebration. His birthday fell on a Saturday and he chose to have a pyjama day, lazing in bed, watching TV, culminating in a birthday tea with a menu he chose. Miraculously the day passed without incident!

Christmas used to pose similar problems, but on a larger scale as traditionally our celebrations included our extended family. In the run-up to his first Christmas with us, Wayne said that he had never been taken to see Father Christmas. We found this hard to believe, given the amount of time he had been in care but he was adamant that he hadn't. So off we went to the local garden centre, which is renowned for its beautiful Christmas grotto. The first difficulty was the huge queue. Wayne found waiting in queues impossible – he would become agitated, then angry and aggressive. We later found out he had been made to stand in a corner for long periods as a punishment. The grotto lived up to our expectation and Wayne was entranced but he couldn't leave anything alone: if it moved he touched it, and as there were electronic moving figures everywhere, it rapidly became dangerous. We feared that one false move from Wayne would bring the whole grotto crashing down. Once he came face to face with Santa he was speechless – not because he was in awe of the man himself but because of the huge array of toys that surrounded him, and from which Wayne was allowed to choose. One by one each of the gifts were picked, only to be discarded seconds later when something more appealing caught Wayne's eye. Eventually we chose a pack of cars for him and hastily ushered him out. Children like Wayne are easily panicked if they are confronted by too many choices.

Our house is usually full on Christmas Eve with friends and neighbours enjoying a drink and mince pie, with the numbers swelling further when the local carol singers and silver band come in for a warming glass of mulled wine. We knew Wayne would never cope with this, so friends and neighbours were invited individually over the Christmas period, and the carol singers and band were served in the street.

On Christmas morning, Wayne came downstairs, ignoring the sack of presents Santa had delivered to his room overnight. He refused to go back to collect them, convinced there would be nothing for him. Eventually, the presents were opened and Wayne stacked them neatly in a pile at one end of the lounge. Spotting some of his friends outside, showing off their new bikes and scooters, he asked if he could join them. We said he could. Wayne went into the hall and collected his old scooter.

'Aren't you going to show your friends your new scooter?'

'Nah, this one's fine.'

Wayne's gifts remained in a neat pile for over a week until I asked why he wasn't playing with them – didn't he like them?

'What's the point?' he replied, 'you'll be selling them soon anyway.'

'Wayne, they are yours, yours to keep. We will never sell

them. That won't happen in this house.'

He grabbed the new scooter and rushed out of the house, 'Hey guys, I've got a new scooter...look!'

Yet again I was in tears.

The following year, Christmas was totally overshadowed by Wayne's school situation. We made him leave the table on Christmas Day because he was refusing to eat anything, saying it was all disgusting. He only had a little turkey and one roast potato (usually his favourite), which he bolted down before he started to make rude comments, poking the food on the table and passing wind loudly. We would normally have made him sit it out, but we decided there were 364 other days when we could do that, and he wasn't going to spoil the meal for the rest of us. We removed him to the lounge. He did his best to ensure that we got indigestion: his provocative behaviour escalated but we sat firm and finished our meal, much to his annoyance.

We reminded each other that it wasn't just major celebrations – even a simple outing was more than Wayne could cope with in the early days. A visit to the zoo, swimming, a day at the beach were all undermined. Even a visit to my sister's house became a real disaster. He opened drawers and cupboards, threw things around and did his best to destroy a wooden ornament my nephew had carved for my sister by "accidentally" knocking into whoever was holding it.

As well as sabotaging treats because he didn't feel he deserved them, he would use similar tactics to get out of, or put an end to, things he simply didn't want to do. It would have been so much easier to have given up and stayed at home, but we did the reverse. The more Wayne spoilt things, the more we did them.

A trip to the supermarket would provide endless entertainment for the other shoppers as Wayne tried to behave outrageously enough for me to take him home. The first time he did this he thought he had "won" as I paid for the few items in the trolley and left. But much to his surprise, the next morning we arrived at the supermarket again.

'I thought we did the shopping yesterday?'

'If you remember, your behaviour was so bad we went home and I didn't get all the things on the list.'

'What, so we've got to do it again?'

'I'm afraid so.' But a few minutes later we were at the checkout.

'Is that it, is that all you wanted?'

'Yes...for today.'

The next day we were back again. 'What the f*** do you think you are doing? We've been here every day!'

'We are practising shopping. When you learn to ride a bike, you do a bit each day until you get the hang of it, and that's what we are doing with shopping, coming every day until you get the hang of it and don't make a fuss.'

'F*** that, get it all now and I'll behave.' He was true to his word and, armed with a pictorial shopping list, Wayne became an enthusiastic shopper. At any hint of difficult behaviour I would only have to mention shopping practice and normal behaviour would be resumed.

We remembered how we slowly started to notice small changes in Wayne's attitude to "good times" and day-to-day activities in general, but he still couldn't accept praise for his achievements. As soon as the words "well done" were out of our mouths, he would do something to prove that he was "bad". We tried everything we could think of but nothing worked. Then one day I remembered a neuro-linguistic programming technique I had learned some years previously. It was called "anchoring" and enabled you to recall a particular state of mind at will by touching a trigger point. I knew that Wayne would be unable to recall a positive state of mind, but perhaps he would remember a word linked to a trigger without me saying the word.

The next time he had a reasonable day I said, 'I would

love to say "well done" to you because you are having a good day, but I know it's too hard for you to hear. I am going to squeeze the lobe of your ear instead.' The next time Wayne did something really well I gently squeezed the lobe of his ear and smiled. 'Thanks, "Mum",' Wayne replied. The ear touch became part of our day-to-day lives; it provided reassurance in situations where Wayne seemed uncertain or anxious. It meant "we care about you" as well as "well done" and remained our alternative to praise.

We started to see small signs that Wayne was starting to trust us. He would knock on our bedroom door to tell us that he had a wet bed. Previously he would either bang on the wall so hard that everything would fall off the shelves and go crashing to our bedroom floor, nearly giving us heart failure, or he would turn up his radio full blast, forcing us to go into his room. He would then say, 'I needed you to change my bed.'

One morning, after a particularly bad outburst the previous evening, Wayne called me to his room. He stood dripping wet with a towel draped around his shoulders; usually he covered up completely, wrapping the towel around himself like a skirt.

'I wanted to say, I was sorry about what I did and said last night.' He looked so vulnerable standing there, and to me it looked like he was saying, 'I know it's OK to stand here like this because I can trust you not to do anything "bad" to me.' I wrapped him in the towel, scooped him into my arms and rocked him like a baby.

Gradually the "Kleenex" moments started to surface: Wayne got upset about an incident with his friends, but cried and recovered quite quickly. Afterwards, as I stuck a plaster on to an injured knee, he said: 'I am pleased you helped me find my feelings because I didn't know them before and it was hard...you are so kind to me and I know it's because you care about me.'

One evening when Tim said goodnight to him, Wayne

asked: 'Are you a ghost?'

'No, I am not a ghost, why?'

'Because I never thought I would have a "dad" like you and I keep thinking you are a ghost and if I open my eyes you will go away.'

And tonight he had managed a whole party and believed he deserved to enjoy himself and have fun.

Tim and I gave ourselves a metaphorical pat on the back. We could have thought our journey had ended but something told us it had only just begun.

11

New beginnings

'Sorry, Tim, I can't go out, I can't celebrate yet, things might go wrong.'

Finally, the long-awaited day arrived, the day when Wayne would be starting at the Castle School. The paperwork from the Department for Children, Schools and Families had taken much longer to come through than had been envisaged. Wayne found himself taking a much longer than anticipated half-term holiday as the local education authority wouldn't allow him to start until the paperwork had arrived. Easter was only two weeks away and some of Wayne's team thought that he should have a slow integration back into school life and start full-time after the Easter break, but Wayne was adamant that it was a "fresh start" and he wanted to go full-time.

After some debate, it had been agreed that the taxi company previously used to transport Wayne to school would be used again. Wayne had a brilliant relationship with the driver and talked about cars with him incessantly. We felt that this would give him some continuity and stability during the forty-minute journey. Tim and I silently held hands as we looked out of the window watching the taxi disappear into the distance; we knew that if this school placement didn't work out there would be no other option than a residential setting for Wayne.

We had planned to go out for a celebratory lunch but found ourselves aimlessly pottering around the house, doing meaningless chores, which could have easily waited until another day.

Finally, I said, 'Sorry, Tim, I can't go out, I can't celebrate yet, things might go wrong.'

Tim was visibly relieved. 'Neither can I...cheese sandwich?'

One by one the days passed and Wayne's positive "can do" attitude remained intact. We were elated but I was falling to pieces. The stresses and strains of the past eighteen months had finally caught up and I needed to take action. Some fifteen years earlier, following the untimely death of my mother, I had counselling from a psychotherapist, Debbie; she had moved out of the area but I still had her contact details. I rang to ask if there was someone in my area she could recommend. As we chatted about my situation, it was as if we had picked up where we had left off: she knew me inside out and we agreed that we could talk on the phone once a week instead of having to find someone new.

The therapeutic fostering scheme made provision for Jane to give "counselling" to Tim, David, Malcolm and to me if it was required, but I didn't feel comfortable with this arrangement. The way I was feeling had been caused in part by the system and Jane belonged to that system. I needed to be able to talk honestly about my emotional state and get it into some kind of perspective, and I couldn't do this with someone I would probably be sitting opposite to at a meeting in the very near future. I felt that independent counselling should have been included in the scheme, but it wasn't and I had to fund it myself.

As these sessions progressed, Debbie helped me to see that I hadn't failed; I had been in an almost impossible position and survived. Over the preceding eighteen months, all the things that had previously helped me maintain my resilience in times of trauma had slowly been eroded away. I had no time to quietly sit and read, attend an art class or meet with friends. My swimming sessions had become Wayne's PE lessons, and I had taken him along on my daily walks with the dogs or paid a local dog walker to take them out so that I could use the time – I thought – more productively. Instead of paying a dog walker, I should have paid for childcare for Wayne so that I had a daily reminder that the world wasn't the chaotic place Wayne created, but a place where beauty and peace still existed.

Debbie asked why we had originally agreed to foster Wayne, what had been our hope and aspirations, had they changed? Clearly they hadn't, and as Wayne continued to flourish at school, we started to regain some semblance of normality in our life.

Malcolm and David were fantastic during this time, taking Wayne out at the weekends as much as they could, giving Tim and me some time together, but what we needed most as a family was some respite. Every avenue our fostering service explored resulted in a dead end. We knew that if we insisted, "someone" would be found, but unless it was the right "someone" the benefits would be eroded by the impact inappropriate care could have on Wayne. And then we would be left to pick up the pieces. We were in a Catch 22 situation.

As the academic year drew to a close, Wayne had been attending the Castle School for nearly three months. Considering he had had very little formal education for nearly 15 months, we felt that just attending full time, being included in the whole curriculum and managing his behaviour most of the time was real progress, but Wayne had a surprise in store. He was very secretive about the plans for the last day of term festivities but did let slip that he had sewn his own costume. His class had been studying Africa and, dressed in the costumes they had made themselves, played African music. Wayne took centre stage, playing both the xylophone and the drum. A child who had never taken part in a school play in his life before – we couldn't believe how much the school had achieved in such a short space of time. Wayne was starting to see a purpose in developing his academic skills to support the practical activities he enjoyed so much. He was popular with staff and pupils alike and really looked forward to each day.

But for us the greatest triumph was that Wayne saw himself as an accepted member of the school community, someone whose thoughts and opinions counted and who was valued for who he was, "warts and all".

That summer, Wayne seemed quite calm and settled. We were able to dramatically reduce the supervision he required when out playing with his friends. As we were in desperate need of a break, we agreed to allow him to join an activity holiday our fostering service had arranged to take place during the summer. One of the social work assistants who had worked with Wayne previously was back from university, so she could accompany him. But we still had reservations. We felt that a whole week would be too much, so it was agreed that Wayne would join the group on the Wednesday and leave with everyone else on the Saturday. For three days we waited for the phone call asking us to come and collect Wayne, but it never came. In fact, we didn't hear a word. We could only assume that all was well. On the Saturday lunchtime Wayne returned completely exhausted but having enjoyed a wonderful time. He had been canoeing, abseiling and had excelled at all physical activities, but in between the activities, keeping him out of trouble had been something of a challenge.

It was evident that some of Wayne's supposed progress

really depended on the stable home and school environment, together with our ever-improving ability to predict and manage his behaviour. If that stability was removed or changed in any way, he would start to revert to his past unhelpful coping strategies.

That autumn, Wayne successfully managed a city break in Prague. However, he still needed to regale us with tales of air disasters on our flights – perhaps this is a clear example of Dan Hughes' theory that the carers' inability to regulate their own emotions in a situation impact on the child: my anxieties about flying have not helped Wayne. Because he also finds it hard to feel settled, away from his familiar environment, it is more difficult to care for him when we are not at home. If only people realised how irritating it is when they ask, 'Have you had a good holiday?' Wayne's ability to have a good holiday is reliant on us working twice as hard mentally to help him feel safe and secure.

Christmas 2008 was one of the best we have had since Wayne's arrival: he approached it with all the excitement of a two-year-old, safe in the knowledge that Santa would be calling on him and a good time would be had by all.

But we are failing miserably in trying to convince him that his safety doesn't depend on him having total command of the TV remote control! It has been an ongoing problem since Wayne arrived with us and one that we have discussed extensively with Wayne's "team", but have yet to find a solution for. If the TV is on he has to have the remote in his hand at all times, repeatedly flipping from channel to channel. If you dare to visit the bathroom or leave the room to make a cup of tea, you can guarantee that when you return another programme will be on the screen with Wayne refusing to turn back again. His anxiety level if you take the remote away from him is out of all proportion.

If we are on holiday, he insists on having the TV on and the remote control in his hand even though he can't understand a word that is being said. If a family trip or outing coincides with, or overlaps, one of his favourite programmes, he will try to persuade us to drive dangerously in order to get home before the programme starts. Why not record the programme, I hear you ask...because in Wayne's world the recording will go wrong, or get switched off, or he won't be allowed to watch it! We have certainly made progress but you can't win them all!

Endpiece

'I can go in a restaurant; I couldn't do that before because I didn't have manners.'

'Is the book nearly finished?' Wayne enquires, peering over my shoulder at the computer screen. It is the summer of 2009 and we have just returned from a two-week holiday in northern Europe. In our absence, my editor has returned the manuscript with a few suggested amendments.

'Yep, it's nearly there,' I reply. 'Are you sure it's OK, you don't mind people reading about "our journey"?'

'No, it's fine, I'm not like that any more...am I?'

'No, you're not, we have come a long way...'

'That's fine then...' Within seconds he has bounded up the stairs and loud music is blaring out of his room.

'Typical teenager,' Tim commented.

'Listen to what he is playing.' The chorus of the song is now blasting out: 'And I'm sorry, so sorry, I'm sorry...'

Wayne still finds it hard to verbalise his emotions but he has become a master at communicating his feelings in other ways: a cup of tea suddenly appearing before you, the offer to do a chore, sidling up for a hug when he needs reassurance, asking one of us to sit and watch TV with him if he has had a bad day. Each afternoon he sends an email home from school telling us how his day has been; it's so much easier to write it down than to tell us.

Wayne is now much more able to regulate his temper and to some extent accept responsibility for his actions. He recently burst the tyre on his bike by riding it inappropriately; he came home and said, 'No bike riding for me until I've saved up. I went a bit stupid on my bike and bust the tyre.'

I pointed out that it would take two weeks to save up, but Wayne just shrugged his shoulders. 'It's my own fault... can I have the key and I will lock it in the garage until it's fixed?'

The next day, Wayne was speechless when Tim came home from work with a new bicycle tyre tucked under his arm. He kept glancing in Tim's direction and we could see him wondering if the tyre was heading his way.

'Here you go, Wayne, the way you accepted responsibility for damaging your tyre and kept a cool head was fantastic; you deserve this.' The biggest smile you have ever seen spread across Wayne's face as he headed off to the garage to retrieve the bike and start the repair.

The move to the Castle School has been one of the best things that has ever happened to Wayne: he is really thriving in the environment, and apart from one day off sick has achieved one hundred per cent attendance over the past fifteen months, a miracle in his educational history. As the 2008/09 academic year drew to a close, he took the leading role in the end of term play and recited his lines with pride and confidence. He stood tall and proud by his teacher's side when his achievements of the year were read out in front of the whole school with family and friends watching. He is able to be a full member of the class in all subjects and no longer needs one-to-one tuition in literacy and numeracy. He excels at the more practical subjects – woodwork and gardening are two of his particular favourites.

Tim and I are delighted that the school has been such a success and worth the relentless fight it took to get him there. But instead of being able to relax and celebrate, and despite reassurances to the contrary by the local education authority, we always fear in the back of our minds that the next Special Educational Needs review could put an end to the funding. We know too that our experience of the education system sadly isn't an isolated case, and that right now there are many, many "Waynes" without a satisfactory school placement.

Wayne is almost unrecognisable from the lad who arrived four-and-a-half years ago; his progress has been beyond anything we could have hoped for when we started on this journey. At present, he appears to have reached a plateau and can't seem to move on to the next level, but of course this could be a hiatus caused by the turmoil of adolescence. Wayne assumed teenage status recently and has immediately slotted into typical teenage behaviour multiplied by ten! Even if he progresses no further, his coming thus far would be a testament to Dan Hughes' methods and parenting with PACE.

Wayne remains on his medication and we know about it very quickly if for any reason we forget to give it to him. We understand that Concerta is used differently for children with attachment difficulties and trauma than for children with ADHD, and that there are no immediate plans to change the prescription. We don't know what the longer-term implications are or the prognosis for adulthood.

This story is about us as much as Wayne and the impact that caring for him has had on our family. David and Malcolm have moved into flats of their own so are playing a much less active role in Wayne's day-to-day care, but they see Wayne as a brother who will always be a part of their lives, no matter what the future holds. They are honest enough to say that having Wayne in our family hasn't always been a positive thing and they have felt helpless at times when they have considered us to be "put upon" by Wayne's team and not given the support we needed or indeed anticipated as part of the therapeutic fostering package. Since his move to the Castle School, Wayne has shown a willingness to try and work through his difficulties; he isn't always able to maintain this but David and Malcolm have a great deal of admiration and respect for his determination and feel proud to have played a part in the process of his recovery.

The fact that no one has been found to replace Joy and Brian and we haven't had any respite for almost two years has put the biggest strain on family life. We used to have two versions of family celebrations: one Wayne-focused and another more relaxed version when Wayne was at respite. Without this, we feel under more pressure to make every occasion work, which increases our anxiety and in turn unsettles Wayne. It's a vicious circle and one we can't see a way out of. It has been so long now since Wayne enjoyed regular periods away from us that we are not sure how he would react if this arrangement were reintroduced.

We have also lost our support during the school holidays. The organised activities are still provided but appropriate one-to-one support for Wayne isn't always available, and being amongst so many unpredictable children, in an environment which has an unfamiliar structure and routine, can send him back into past behaviour patterns. Tim finds himself having to take time off work in order for us to have any time together. After some wrangling we are now paid "compensation" for our lack of respite, but this doesn't save our sanity.

The question we often ask ourselves is, would we do it again? Seeing the change in Wayne, we feel proud of what we have achieved. Sometimes we feel we could have achieved so much more and without the huge emotional cost, if the scheme had been better resourced and funded. When we undertook Wayne's care, we planned to reach a point when perhaps we could consider doing the same for another child. But the lack of resources and having to fight for what should be Wayne's given right has left us feeling that we would never go down this road again unless the required resources were in place. This saddens us because we feel we have gained so many skills and so much understanding that we would have more to offer next time.

We are in no doubt as to the effectiveness of Dan Hughes' methods, but at times have found them a challenge to fit into family life; we certainly wouldn't have wanted to try and undertake this journey if David and Malcolm had been younger, as the impact on their life would have been just too great. Although Dan Hughes' methods have formed the basis for the way we have worked with Wayne, we have also taken a very holistic approach: using relaxation techniques, reiki, reflexology and elements from Neuro-Linguistic Programming, Non-Violent Communication and Solution-Focused Therapy. We have also drawn a great deal of inspiration from some of the other schools of thought on working with traumatised children, particularly the work of Kate Cairns. We firmly believe that, as each child is such an individual, using only one way of working could hinder their progress and healing.

Who knows what challenges adolescence will bring for Wayne and for us. Will he ever be able to live independently or will he always need some additional support? Whatever the outcome, we are committed to being a part of his life for as long as we are able.

Just as it seems that the book is finally completed, Wayne comes down from his room, leaving the music blaring away in the background.

'Shall we take the dogs out and have a picnic by the

river...you could bring the book and read it to me again.'

'Would you like to hear it again before I send it off, just to make sure it's OK?'

'Yeah – I'll get my boots.'

The music is turned off, a picnic hastily prepared and the dogs can't believe their luck – two walks in one day. We settle ourselves by the river and I start to read, while Wayne munches a sandwich. When he has finished eating he calls Holly, our black Labrador, and rests his head on her as he continues to listen. Every now and then he shakes his head in disbelief as he hears the account of some of his behaviours. I don't read the extracts about how Wayne's behaviour made us feel, just about the incidents themselves and Wayne's progress.

Silently, raindrops begin to appear on the paper and we have to gather our things and head home. As we climb the hill back to the village, Wayne takes my hand but keeps looking straight ahead.

'You've changed me a lot.'

'We've done it together, you can't make someone change – they have to be willing to make changes too. It's easier to stay the same than it is to change.'

'Yeah, but I can do so many things now... I can go in a restaurant, I couldn't do that because I didn't have manners...I know how to behave, so I can go to lots of places...I can go out and be like a normal person...I am getting good at reading and things so I will be able to get a job...'

'Yes, there have been some *big* changes, you've worked hard.'

'You've given me a chance...a chance of a new life, I didn't have a chance before but now you've given me one...' Barely audible above the sound of the leaves rustling in the breeze and the pattering rain, Wayne mutters, 'Thank you' as he runs off to rejoin Holly.

Wayne has said it all – none of us know what the future

holds for him, but we have given him a chance.

As I watch him disappear up the hill, now with both dogs lolloping along beside him, I think how anyone observing him would just see a lad enjoying an early autumn walk, the scars of his past hidden.

Beautiful child

The sun shines on your beautiful face
Your complexion pale and unblemished
Skin so smooth...perfect
Beautiful child, beautiful child

Your eyes so clear and blue,
Dance seemingly so full of joy
Your smile so big and bright
Laughter ripples as you run
Beneath the autumn trees
Beautiful child, beautiful child

But looks deceive, beneath the cloak
Of joy and laughter lies the turmoil of your mind
Memories of a childhood snatched away
By those a babe should trust
Beautiful child, beautiful child

A leaf floats down
You catch it in your open palm
Tree and child become as one
A child whose mind was once undone
Beautiful child, beautiful child

Your winter has been long and hard
With snow and sleet and rain
Your branches have been wrenched apart
But you are nearly whole again

People pass but all they see is
A boy catching leaves
As they fall from the tree
Beautiful child, beautiful child

Lorna Miles, 2009

Bibliography

Bowlby J (1969) *Attachment*, vol 1, *Attachment and Loss* trilogy, New York, NY: Basic Books

Cairns K (2002) *Attachment, Trauma and Resilience: Therapeutic caring for children*, London: BAAF

Hobday A (2001) 'Timeholes: a useful metaphor when explaining unusual or bizarre behaviour in children who have moved families', *Clinical Child Psychology and Psychiatry*, 6:1, pp 41—47

Hughes D (2006) *Building the Bonds of Attachment: Awakening love in deeply troubled children* (2nd edn), Lanham, MD: Jason Aronson

Hughes D (2007) *Attachment-Focused Family Therapy*, New York, NY: WW Norton & Co

Hughes D (2009) *Attachment-Focused Parenting: Effective strategies to care for children*, New York, NY: WW Norton & Co

Pannapadipo PP (2005) *Little Angels: Life as a novice monk in Thailand*, London: Arrow Books

Sher B (1998) *Self-Esteem Games: 300 fun activities that make children feel good about themselves*, San Francisco, CA: Jossey Bass